Nov. 3. 08

To!

Eunice Noh
&
June Noh

Scholastic Children's

Atlas of Canada

Scholastic Canada Ltd.

New York • Toronto • London • Auckland • Sydney • Mexico City • New Delhi • Hong Kong • Buenos Aires

Library and Archives Canada Cataloguing in Publication
Éditions Québec Amérique
Scholastic children's atlas of Canada [cartographic material]/
Québec Amérique.

ISBN 0-439-97434-8
1. Canada — Maps for children. 2. Children's atlases. 3. Atlases, Canadian. I. Title. II. Title: Children's atlas of Canada.

G1115.E34 2006 j912'.71 C2006-900656-3

Scholastic Children's Atlas of Canada
was created and produced by
QA International
329 de la Commune St. West
3rd floor
Montreal, Quebec
H2Y 2E1 Canada
T 514.499.3000 F 514.499.3010

Published by
Scholastic Canada Ltd.
604 King Street West
Toronto, Ontario
M5V 1E1 Canada

10 9 8 7 6 5 4 3 2 1 Printed and bound in Singapore 06 07 08 09 10 11 12

Editorial Director
François Fortin
Caroline Fortin
Editor
Martine Podesto
Chief Writer
Stéphanie Lanctôt
Writer
Marie-Anne Legault
Graphic Designer
Josée Noiseux
Layout
Émilie Corriveau
Mathieu Douville
Danielle Quinty
Art Directors
Anouk Noël
Jocelyn Gardner
Illustrators
Manuela Bertoni
Alain Lemire
Raymond Martin
Photo Acquisition
Gilles Vézina
Project Manager
Odile Perpillou
Cartographer
François Turcotte-Goulet
Fact Checking
Julie Cailliau
Translator
Donna Vekteris
Proofreading
Veronica Schami Editorial Services
Production
Guylaine Houle
Prepress
Kien Tang
Karine Lévesque
Sophie Pellerin

Photo credits

p. 18 Mountain © A. Badjura; **p. 18** Pacific dogwood © J. Tringali; **p. 18** Steller's jay © G. Coffman; **p. 19** Burgess shale © S. Earle; **p. 20** Young Asian © A. Maw; **p. 21** Victoria © A. Maw; **p. 21** Vancouver © S. Hawkins; **p. 22** Buffalo jump © C. J. White; **p. 22** Wild rose © B. Reynolds; **p. 22** Petrified wood © PD Photo.org; **p. 22** Great horned owl © G. Lavaty; **p. 23** Banff National Park © A. Badjura; **p. 24** Calgary Stampede © Calgary Stampede; **p. 24** Jasper © D. Wong; **p. 25** Blackfoot of Alberta © A. Klaw; **p. 25** Edmonton © J. Dailey-O'Cain; **p. 25** Calgary © G. Hebert; **p. 26** Athabasca Sand Dunes © R. Wright; **p. 26** Sharp-tailed grouse, Western red lily and Potash © Saskatchewan Government Relations; **p. 28** Agricultural machinery © H.Dreyer; **p. 29** RCMP © V.K. Chan / ArcticCircle Photography; **p. 29** Young Ukrainians © Saskatchewan Centennial 2005 / designed and created by M. Greschner; **p. 29** Saskatoon © J. Mineer; **p. 29** Regina © D. Shaler; **p. 30** Great gray owl © R. Brady; **p. 31** Polar bear © E. Bouvier; **p. 31** Piping plover © G. Prince; **p. 32** Louis Riel statue © N. Giesbrecht; **p. 32** Golden Boy © C. Turner; **p. 32** Brandon © Economic Development Brandon; **p. 32** Train © D. Hagen; **p. 33** Winnipeg © E. Bouvier; **p. 34** White trillium © P. Stewart; **p. 34** Amethyst © D. Dyet; **p. 34** Common loon © D. Backlund; **p. 35** Niagara Falls © J-M. Boutellier/http://Planetphoto.free.fr; **p. 36** Girl with apple © P. Hoffmann; **p. 36** Caribana © S. Noseworthy; **p. 37** Parliament Hill © M. Fiorillo; **p. 37** Toronto © V. Ghiea; **p. 38** Wild iris © J. Stahlman; **p. 38** Snowy owl © J. Laurencelle; **p. 39** Magdalen island © Tourisme Îles de la Madeleine/M. Bonato; **p. 39** Mauricie National Park © R. Zeithammer; **p. 40** Young Quebecers © J. Noiseux; **p. 41** Maple syrup © C. Chevalier; **p. 41** Quebec City © C. Green; **p. 41** Montreal © F. Fortin; **p. 42** Black-capped chickadee © H. Cummins, Miami University; **p. 43** Bouctouche Dune © A. Desruisseaux; **p. 43** Bay of Fundy © New Brunswick Department of Tourism and Parks; **p. 44** Acadian culture © Le pays de la Sagouine; **p. 45** Moncton © Moncton Tourism; **p. 45** Fredericton © City of Fredericton Tourism Division; **p. 46** Osprey © A. Fossé; **p. 46** Stilbite © David K. Joyce; **p. 47** Cape Breton Highlands National Park © C. Green; **p. 47** Sable Island © M.Tuttle; **p. 48** Port-Royal © D. Mercer; **p. 49** Halifax Citadel © Destination Halifax/D. Towler; **p. 49** Halifax © D. Towsey; **p. 49** Scottish folklore © M. Holmes; **p. 50** Rusty ground © N. Thorne; **p. 50** Lady's slipper © K. Taylor; **p. 50** Blue jay © G. Lazzaro; **p. 51** PEI National Park © D. MacPhee; **p. 51** Beach © B. Carnevale; **p. 52** Province House © S. Godfrey; **p. 52** Mi'kmaq culture © Lennox Island cultural centre; **p. 53** Green Gables © A. Hines; **p. 53** Charlottetown © M. Buchanan; **p. 53** Confederation Bridge © D. Lee; **p. 54** Pitcher plant © R. Lortie; **p. 54** Atlantic puffin © D. Shaw/Fair Isle Bird Observatory; **p. 54** Labradorite © J.M. Oldham/OldhaMedia; **p. 55** Iceberg © Corel; **p. 55** Gros Morne National Park © M. White; **p. 56** L'Anse aux Meadows © M. White; **p. 57** Demasduit © National Archives of Canada; **p. 57** St. John's © J. Zhang; **p. 57** Hibernia © Hibernia Public Affairs; **p. 58** Lazulite © D. Weinrich; **p. 58** Fireweed © M. Skalitzky; **p. 59** Northern lights © Courtesy of Newfoundland and Labrador Tourism; **p. 59** Midnight sun © V.K. Chan/ArcticCircle Photography; **p. 59** Gyrfalcon © R. Brady; **p. 59** Purple saxifrage © www.markblomster.com; **p. 59** Rock ptarmigan © S. Caron; **p. 60** Whitehorse © R. Tanaka; **p. 60** Yellowknife © Northwest Territories Resources Wildlife and Economic Development; **p. 61** Iqaluit © V.K. Chan/ArcticCircle Photography; **p. 61** Dene © Northwest Territories Resources Wildlife and Economic Development; **p. 61** Young Inuit © V. Saltzman **p. 62** First Canadian Place © Wikipedia/Simon P.

The arms of Canada were reproduced with the permission of the Government of Canada, 2006.

The provincial and territorial shields were reproduced with the permission of the corresponding governments, 2006.

Contents

What is a map?

A map is a drawing of a particular area, usually seen from above. A map makes it possible to look at a city, for example, as if you were a bird flying overhead. You can see the position of the streets and where the important buildings are. You can also find a specific place at a glance. A map is a must for people who visit a place for the first time. It helps them to move around without getting lost. A map can also supply information about the particular features of an area and its inhabitants.

1. This image shows us a city the way we would see it from a hilltop or a skyscraper. Some streets are hidden by buildings.

2. This image shows us the same city, but from higher up — the way a bird in flight or an airplane pilot would see it. All the buildings and streets are now visible. It is this point of view that is used to draw maps.

3. It is difficult to describe an area down to the tiniest detail. This is why mapmakers rely on symbols. Symbols are simple pictures that represent real, more complex elements. The meaning of each symbol used on the map is explained in a special list called a legend.

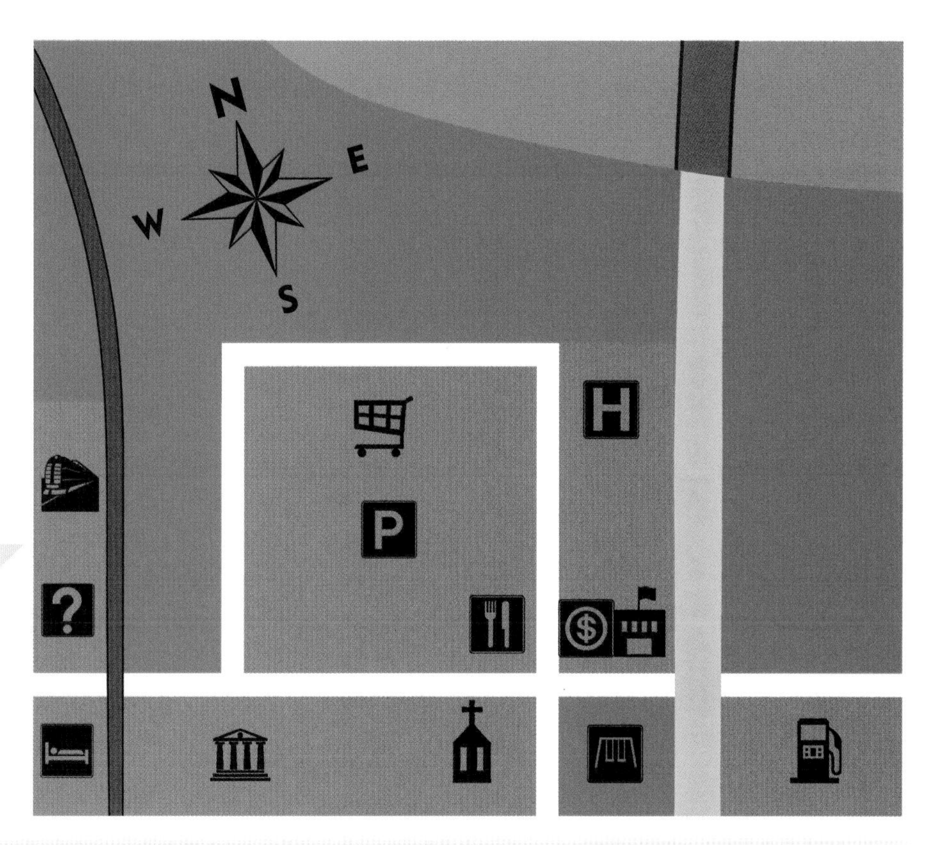

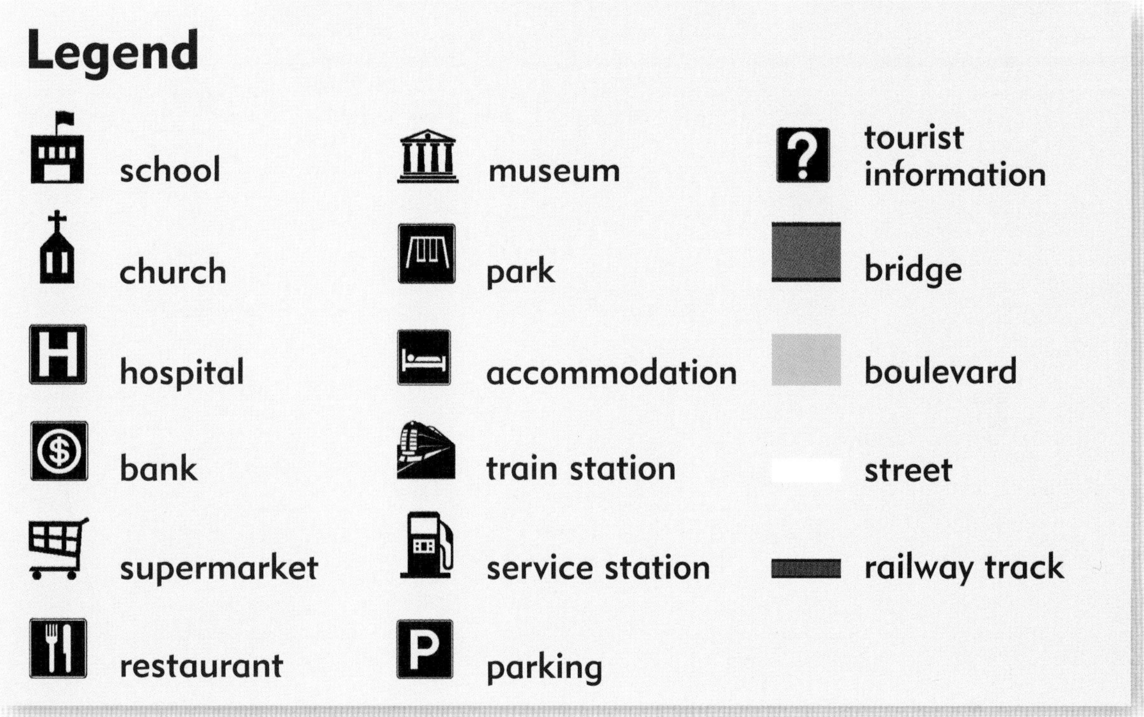

A map made to scale

All the elements represented on a map are much smaller than in real life. Their size in relation to each other, however, is the same. We say that a map is drawn "to scale." This means that when a street on a map is twice as long as another street, we know that it is twice as long in real life, too.

The compass rose

Most maps include a compass rose. A compass rose is a drawing shaped like a star that points north, south, east and west.

To each his own map

Drivers, tourists and hikers need maps to help them find their way. They don't, however, need the same kind of information. That is why there are different kinds of maps. Maps for drivers mainly show the road network. The maps that tourists use focus on an area's main attractions. Maps for hikers describe the location of trails, streams and mountains. There are maps for every interest and type of work. The astronomer uses maps that show the position of the stars, while the meteorologist works with maps that show weather patterns.

A road map

A road map has a variety of symbols to represent expressways, highways and secondary roads.

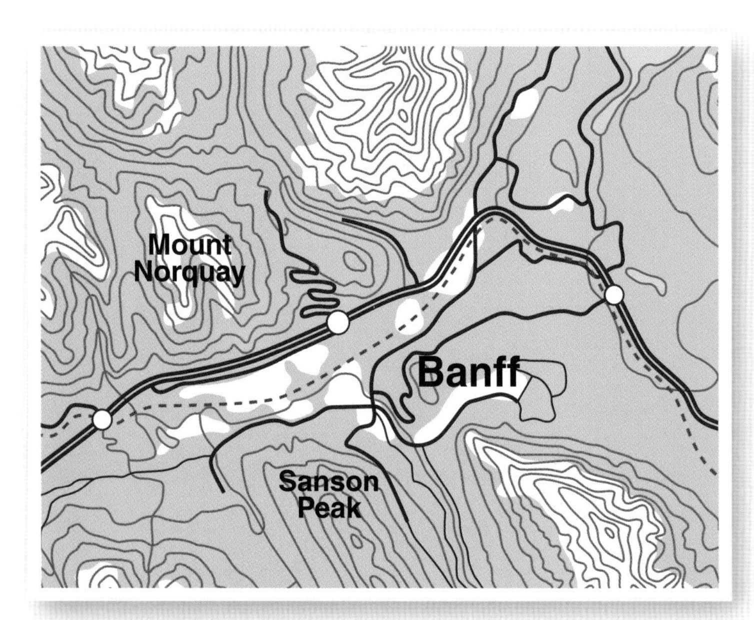

A topographic map

A topographic map shows the position of natural features in the landscape. Mountains are represented by a series of rings that become smaller as the land rises.

A sky chart

A sky chart shows the position of the stars. Long ago, people traced imaginary drawings in the sky, connecting groups of stars. These are called constellations. These reference points helped sailors find their way at sea.

Drawing Earth

Cartographers are people who draw maps. Sometimes they need to create a map of the world. How do cartographers manage to draw our round planet on a flat sheet of paper? There are a number of techniques for doing this, but none of them is perfect. On a map of the world, the continents and the distances that separate them are always distorted in some places.

Earth as a globe

The terrestrial globe is a reliable representation of our planet. This ball is bulky, however, and can't be put into a book!

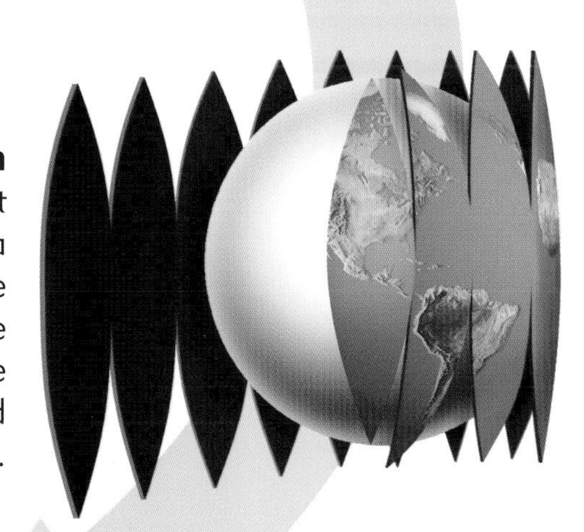

Peeling Earth

One technique that makes it possible to represent Earth on a flat surface is to "peel" the globe the way we peel the sections of an orange. The "skin" of the globe is then laid flat to make a map.

A map of the world

The globe's surface, when laid flat, contains many empty spaces. Cartographers fill in these blank areas by extending the oceans and the continents. This makes some parts of the world appear larger than they really are.

An atlas

An atlas is a collection of maps put into a book. The atlas gets its name from an ancient Greek legend. Atlas was a giant who tried to fight against the Greek gods. The gods punished Atlas by making him carry Earth and the heavens on his shoulders.

How do I use this atlas?

In this atlas, each province and territory is represented by two maps. The first map shows you the natural features of each province. You'll discover the plants and animals that live there, the particular details of its landscape and the wealth of its underground ***minerals***. The second map shows you how Canadians live. You'll learn about the ***industries*** that are important to each region, where major cities and points of interest are located and how people live day to day.

Where am I?

This globe makes it easy to quickly locate a province or territory in Canada.

Climate and vegetation

Climate varies from one region to another. It influences the ***vegetation*** that grows in a region and the animals that live there. In this atlas, maps of the provinces and territories show the types of vegetation found in Canada.

Ice and snow

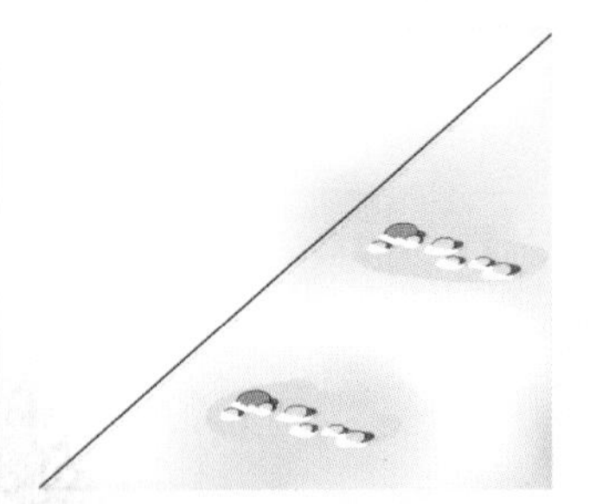

Canada's northern regions are covered with ice and snow. The climate is so cold that no vegetation grows here.

Tundra

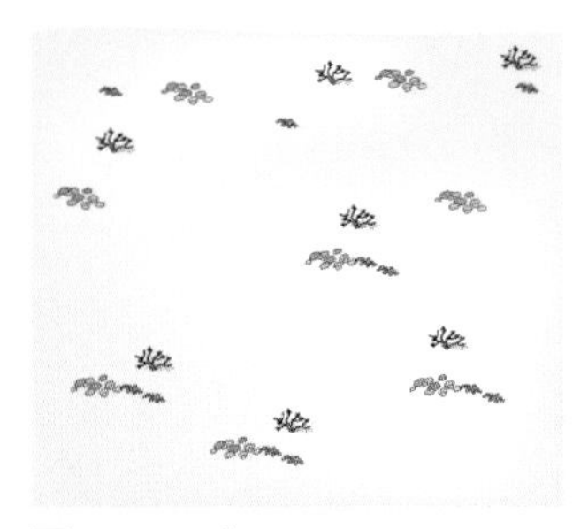

The tundra is a region with no trees. Only moss, lichen and some small shrubs grow in these regions.

Taiga

The taiga is a forest that is a combination of tundra and boreal forest. It is made up of scattered ***conifers***.

Boreal forest

The boreal forest is made up of conifers, which include fir, spruce and pine trees.

Mixed forest

The mixed forest is a combination of boreal and leafy forest. It is made up of leafy trees and conifers.

Leafy forest

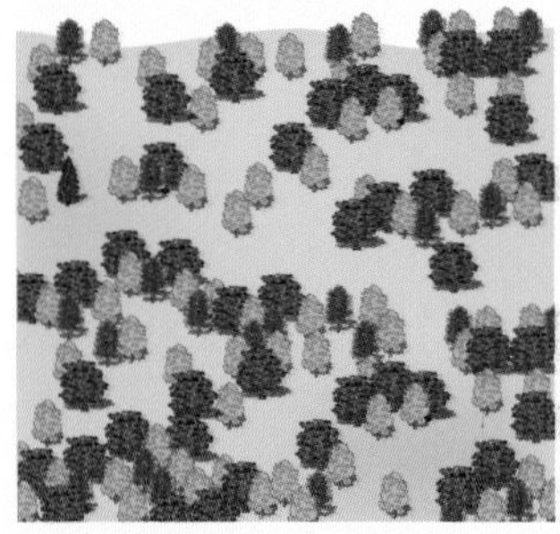

The leafy forest is made up of trees such as maple and birch which have leaves that fall in the autumn.

Prairies

The prairies are large, grass-covered plains. Trees are rarely found here.

Mountains

Mountains may be rounded, or capped by tall peaks with steep slopes. Some peaks are so high that no vegetation grows here.

What is it?

This legend will help you understand what the symbols on each map represent.

capital of Canada

capital of a province or territory

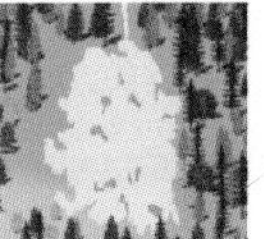
lake

river

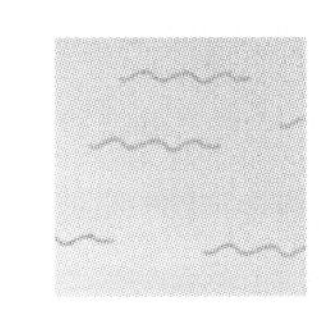
ocean or sea

waterfall

mountains

crops

beef industry

dairy industry

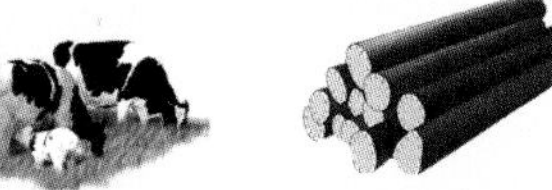
forest industry

mining

oil drilling

manufacturing

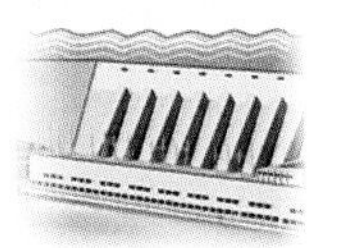
hydroelectric dam

fishing

major airport

city

medium city

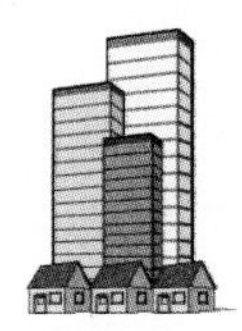
large city

Trans-Canada Highway

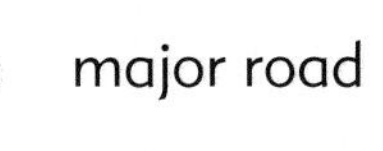
major road

railway

Is it very far?

You can calculate the distance between two places on a map with the help of a scale. This example represents 300 kilometres.

In this atlas, a scale is provided for each province and for the territories. To measure, you will need some string and a pen.

1. Place the string on a map to measure a distance you would like to know. Mark the string with a pen.
2. Using the scale on that page, measure your length of string to find out how many kilometres it represents.

1 km (kilometre) = 1000 m (metres)

Where do people live?

Some regions in a province or territory are more populated than others. The more houses that are grouped together, the more inhabitants there are in the region.

What does it mean?

Some words in this atlas may need explaining. They have been printed in ***bold and italic*** letters. You can find these words listed with their meanings on the Terminology page at the end of the book (page 64).

Emblems

Just like Canada, every province and territory has its own emblems. They may include a flower, a bird, a tree or even a mineral.

Flower	Bird	Tree	Mineral

Around the world

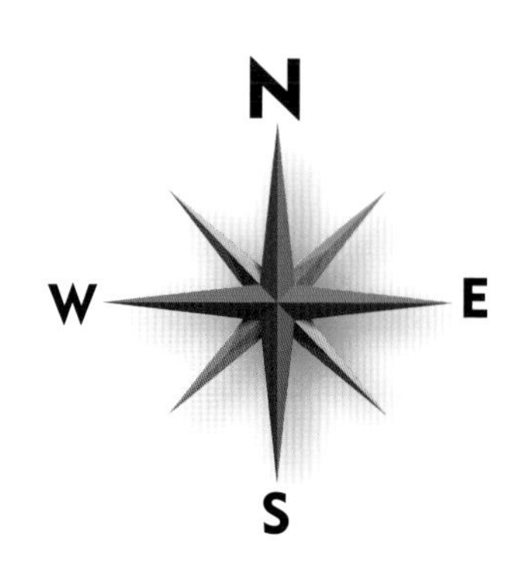

Looking at Earth from space, we can see that most of the planet's surface is not land, but water. This water forms the world's oceans. There are five of them: the Pacific, Atlantic, Indian, Arctic and Southern oceans. The oceans surround land masses called continents. They are North America, South America, Europe, Africa, Asia, Oceania and Antarctica.

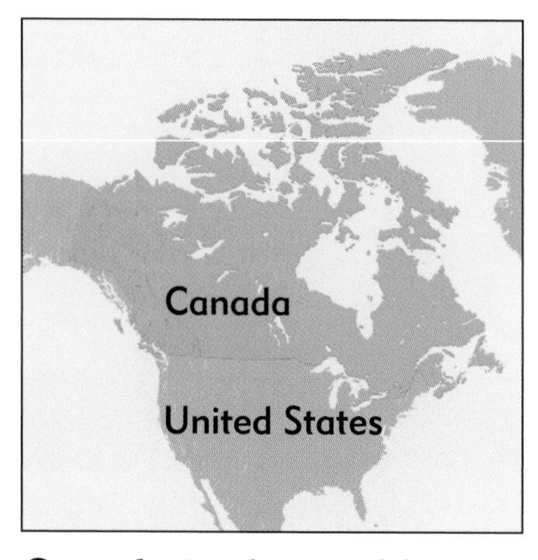

Canada in the world

Canada is a country situated in Earth's northern hemisphere. It is part of North America. Canada is bounded by the Atlantic Ocean to the east, the Pacific Ocean to the west and the Arctic Ocean to the north. Canada is bordered by another country, the United States, to the south.

Arctic Ocean

The **Arctic Ocean** is situated at the extreme north of the planet. Part of this ocean is covered in floating ice.

North America is the second-largest continent. It includes Central America, which joins the continent to South America.

Pacific Ocean

The **Pacific Ocean** is the largest ocean in the world. It covers more than one-third of the planet.

South America contains the largest tropical forest on the planet: Amazonia.

Antarctica is covered in ice. It is situated at the extreme southern end of Earth. Antarctica is the coldest place on the planet.

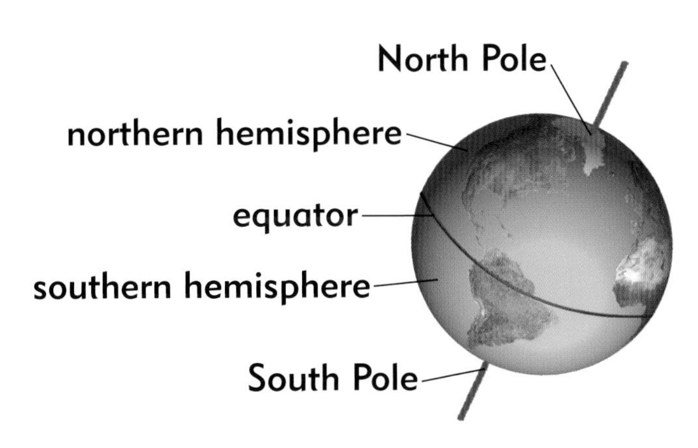

The northern and southern hemispheres

Earth looks a little like a spinning top. The South Pole is at the bottom end of this "top" and the North Pole is at the top end. The equator encircles the planet halfway between the two poles. It divides the world into two parts: the northern hemisphere and the southern hemisphere.

Many countries

Humans have divided the continents into countries. There are 192 countries in the world. Each one has its own government and laws. Borders are imaginary lines that separate the countries. Canada shares a long border with the United States.

Europe is often regarded as a continuation of the Asian continent. It is separated from Asia by the Ural Mountains.

Ural Mountains

Europe

Asia

Africa

Asia is the largest continent. It is also the most populated. More than half of the people on the planet live here.

northern hemisphere

southern hemisphere

Indian Ocean

The **Indian Ocean** lies between Africa and Oceania. Its waters are the warmest in the world.

Oceania

Oceania is the smallest continent. It consists of islands scattered in the Pacific Ocean. The largest of these islands is Australia.

Atlantic Ocean

The **Atlantic Ocean** is the second-largest ocean. It separates North and South America from Europe and Africa.

Africa is the hottest continent. It includes the Sahara Desert, which is the largest desert in the world.

Southern Ocean

The **Southern Ocean** (or Antarctic Ocean) surrounds Antarctica. It is a freezing cold ocean with fierce winds.

Antarctica

My country, Canada

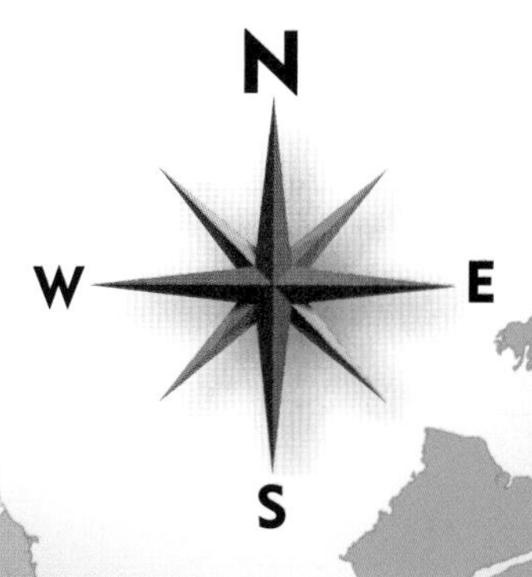

Canada is the second-largest country in the world. Its landscape includes vast stretches of forest as well as countless lakes and rivers. Canada can be divided into five great regions: the West Coast, the Prairies, the Great Lakes and the St. Lawrence River, the Atlantic Region and the Northern Territories. For 400 years, people have been coming from many other countries to make Canada their new home. Canada's Native people, its first inhabitants, now represent only a small portion of the population. The country is divided into 10 provinces and three territories, and the main languages spoken are English and French.

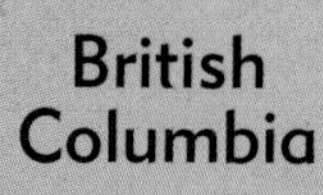

Origin of the name "Canada"

The name "Canada" comes from *kanata*, an Iroquois word that means "village." More than 450 years ago, the Iroquois who welcomed French explorer Jacques Cartier used this word, trying to point out to him where their settlement was located. As a result, Cartier gave this name to the entire area.

I am Canadian

Canada has more than 30 million inhabitants. Most people live in cities in the southern part of the country, where the ***climate*** is warmer.

The **West Coast** is the region where Canada meets the Pacific Ocean. Tall ***mountain ranges*** run through parts of British Columbia, Alberta and the Yukon.

The **Prairies** are vast plains covering large parts of Alberta, Saskatchewan and Manitoba. Huge amounts of grain are grown here.

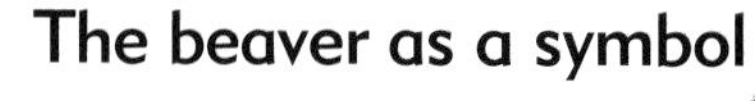

The beaver as a symbol

The beaver is an official emblem of Canada. The beaver fur trade played an important role in the country's history.

Canada's motto

From sea to sea

What's the climate?

Northern Canada has a polar ***climate***. Temperatures here are very cold. Southern Canada has a temperate climate. The temperatures here are variable, and there are four very distinct seasons: summer, fall, winter and spring.

Yukon, the Northwest Territories and Nunavut are the **Northern Territories**. For most of the year, the ground here is frozen and covered in snow.

New Brunswick, Nova Scotia, Prince Edward Island, and Newfoundland and Labrador border on the Atlantic Ocean. Together they make up the **Atlantic Region**.

The capital of Canada

The Canadian Parliament is located in Ottawa. This is where the country's leaders meet and pass laws.

The **Great Lakes and the St. Lawrence River** form a basin that waters Ontario and Quebec. More than half of all Canadians live in these two provinces.

The maple leaf

There is a maple leaf in the centre of the Canadian flag. Maple trees are highly prized. Canadians appreciate the quality of the wood, the sweet taste of the sap and the beautiful red leaves in the fall.

The first inhabitants

It is thought that Canada's earliest inhabitants came from Asia. Thousands of years ago, the level of the oceans was lower than it is today. This would have allowed Asians to cross over from their continent to North America, walking on a strip of land that today is covered by water. They would have then scattered across North America to form different nations. Each nation adapted to the ***climate*** and natural ***resources*** of its own region. Nations living in the same region developed a very similar way of life.

Six large regions

Before the Europeans arrived, Canada's Native inhabitants were scattered over six large regions: the Arctic, Subarctic, Pacific Coast, Plateau, Plains and Eastern Woodlands.

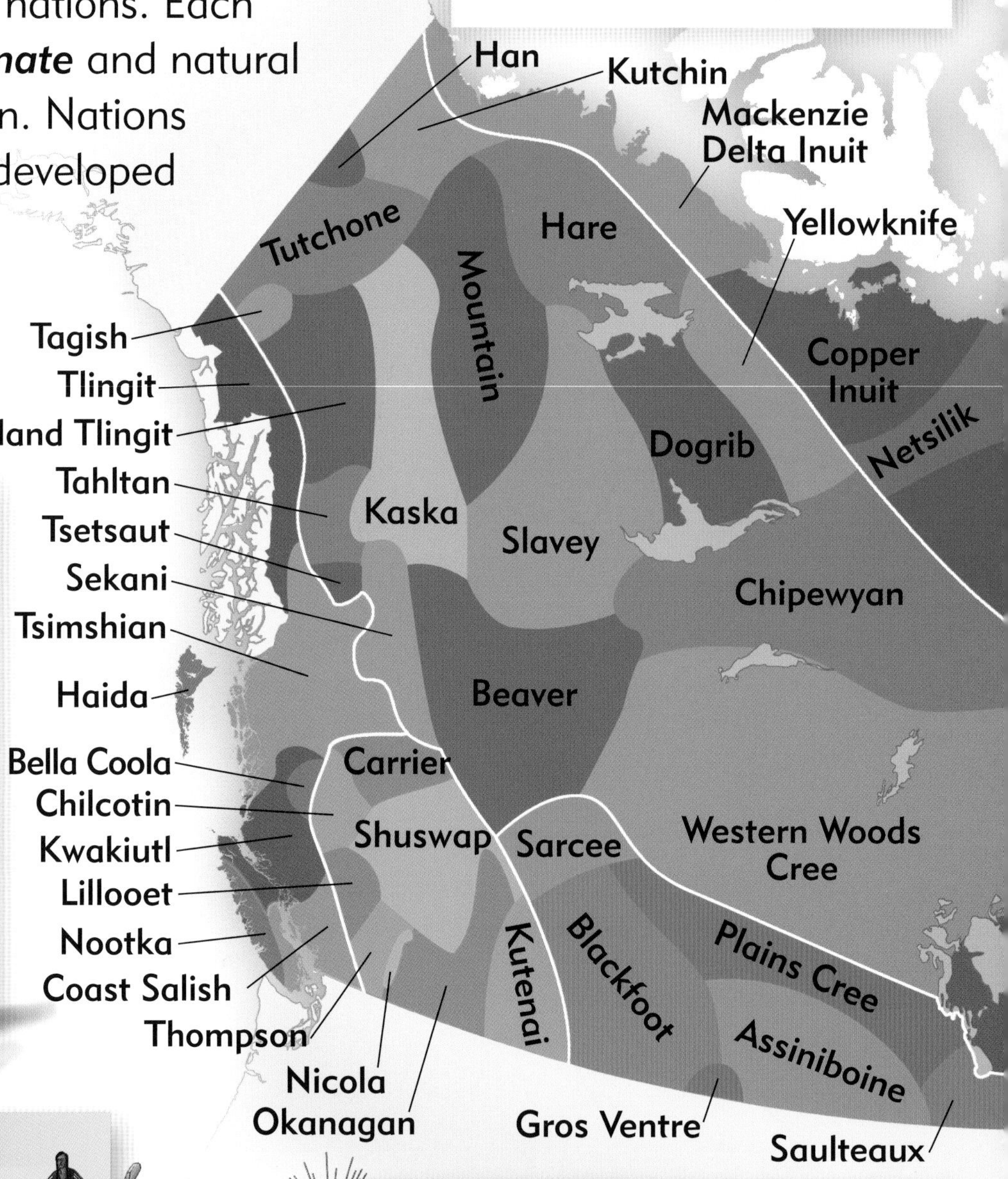

Han
Kutchin
Mackenzie Delta Inuit
Tutchone
Hare
Yellowknife
Mountain
Tagish
Tlingit
Inland Tlingit
Copper Inuit
Dogrib
Netsilik
Tahltan
Tsetsaut
Sekani
Tsimshian
Kaska
Slavey
Chipewyan
Haida
Beaver
Bella Coola
Chilcotin
Kwakiutl
Lillooet
Nootka
Coast Salish
Thompson
Nicola
Okanagan
Carrier
Shuswap
Sarcee
Western Woods Cree
Kutenai
Blackfoot
Plains Cree
Assiniboine
Gros Ventre
Saulteaux

Pacific Coast fishermen

Pacific Coast peoples lived mainly by catching salmon. The giant cedars of the coastal forest provided them with wood to build their longhouses and massive canoes as well as their totem poles. These poles were carved tree trunks that told the story of their families.

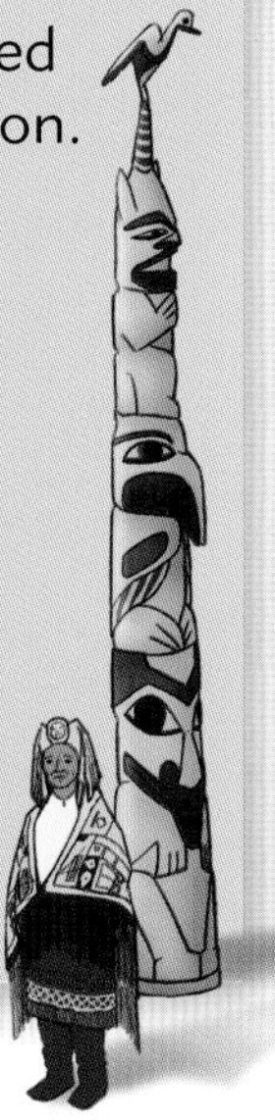

Peoples of the Plateau

The Plateau peoples settled in a large valley surrounded by mountains and crisscrossed by rivers. They fished for salmon in the rivers and hunted animals, like the mountain goat. In winter, they dug pit houses, which were underground except for the roofs.

Plains buffalo hunters

The lives of the Plains peoples revolved around the bison, or buffalo. They ate buffalo meat and used the bones and horns to make tools and utensils. Buffalo skin was made into clothing and cone-shaped tents, called *tipis*.

Native inventions

The first inhabitants created many useful implements, including the toboggan, the komatik and snowshoes, for travelling on snow; and two kinds of lightweight boats — the canoe and the kayak — for travelling on water. The Inuit designed the anorak, a warm winter coat with a hood. The game of lacrosse, a team sport, is also a Native invention.

Teaching

The Native peoples in Canada did not have written languages. Children learned about their people's history and traditions by listening to stories and legends told by the oldest members of the ***community***.

Arctic Inuit

The Inuit inhabited the North, on the shores of the Arctic Ocean. There were very few plants to be found in this extremely cold ***climate***. To survive, the Inuit fished and hunted marine animals, like seals and whales. In winter, many Inuit built *iglus*, which are shelters made from blocks of ice.

Subarctic hunters

The inhabitants of this region lived by hunting animals, like caribou and beaver, and gathering wild fruits. They were constantly on the move in search of food. In the summer, they travelled in canoes made of tree bark. In the winter, they travelled on the snow using snowshoes.

Eastern Woodlands peoples

The Native peoples of the Eastern Woodlands lived on the fertile land bordering the Great Lakes and the St. Lawrence River. Many of them settled in villages and were farmers. The Iroquois built longhouses made of wood and covered in bark. They grew corn, squash and beans.

New arrivals, new challenges

A timeline of events

Europeans began to explore North America a thousand years ago, when Viking sailors reached the island of Newfoundland. Five hundred years later, Europeans "discovered" North America once again, while searching for the shortest route to Asia. Explorer John Cabot, sailing under the English flag, reached the shores of Newfoundland or possibly Cape Breton. One hundred years after that, the French became the first Europeans to settle permanently in Canada.

1837
Groups of colonists rebel against British rule. They want more say in how their government is run. The rebellions are crushed by British soldiers.

1793
Explorer Alexander Mackenzie crosses Canada from east to west and reaches the Pacific Ocean.

1783
The Americans win their independence after years of fighting the British. The Loyalists — Americans who are faithful to Great Britain — escape and help to populate the British ***colonies*** in the south of Canada.

1858
Thousands of people rush to the Fraser River in western Canada in search of gold. Their numbers will help to populate British Columbia.

1867
Four colonies — New Brunswick, Nova Scotia, Quebec and Ontario — unite to form a country called the Dominion of Canada. To this day, Canadians celebrate the event as a national holiday on July 1.

1869
In the western prairies, the Native peoples and the Metis, who are of mixed Native and European parentage, rebel against settlers arriving from the East. The Canadian government sends in troops to crush the rebellion.

1999
The Canadian government creates a third territory in the North, called Nunavut. This territory is governed mainly by the Inuit.

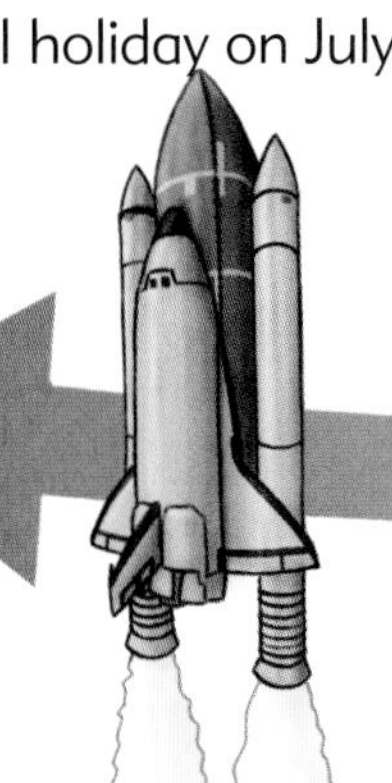

1984
Astronaut Marc Garneau is the first Canadian in space.

1959
Construction of the St. Lawrence Seaway is completed. Large ships can now sail all the way from the Atlantic Ocean to the Great Lakes.

1534
Navigator Jacques Cartier explores the Gulf of St. Lawrence and takes possession of Canada in the name of the King of France.

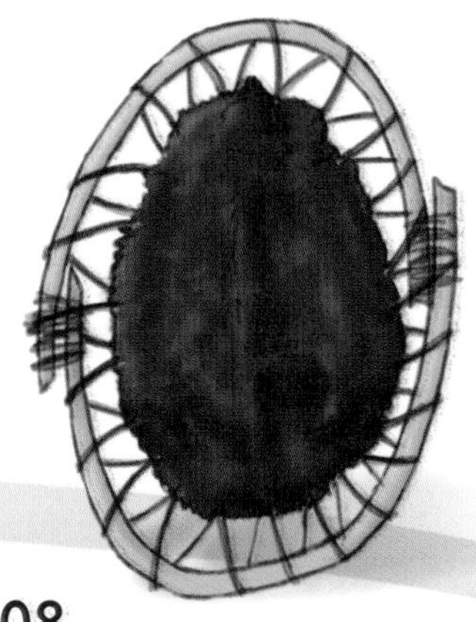

1608
French merchants come to settle on the shores of the St. Lawrence River and build Quebec City. These ***colonists*** trade with the Native people, exchanging useful metal items for beaver furs.

1670
The English establish the Hudson's Bay Company to trade furs with the Native peoples around Hudson Bay.

1755
The French colonists (the Acadians) who have settled in Nova Scotia are driven from their land and forced to leave by the British, who have taken possession of the territory.

1763
The British emerge as the winners in a long war with France. They take possession of the entire Canadian territory. The French colonists of Quebec are allowed to keep their land but are now under British rule.

1885
A railway crosses Canada, linking the Atlantic Ocean to the Pacific Ocean. The settling of the Canadian West speeds up, thanks to this rapid and practical new way to travel.

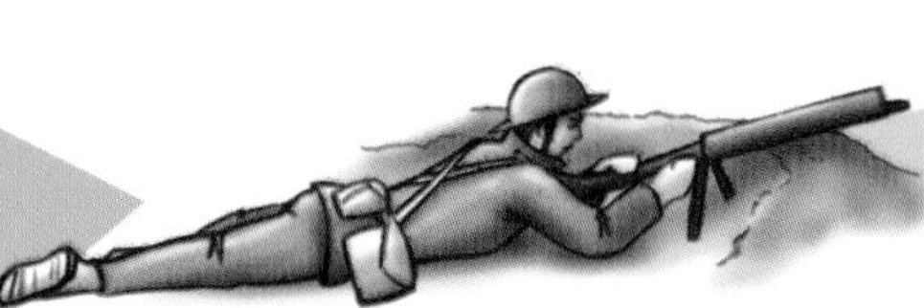

1914
World War I breaks out in Europe. Hundreds of thousands of soldiers from Canada and Newfoundland cross the Atlantic to fight alongside the British.

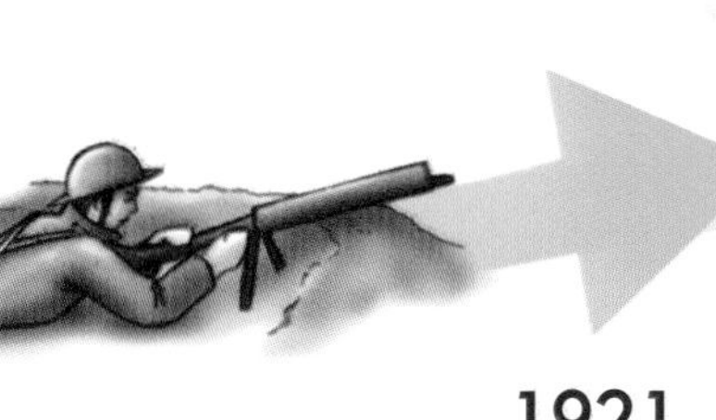

1921
Two Canadians, Dr. Frederick Banting and medical student Charles Best, discover insulin, a medicine that saves the lives of people with diabetes.

1936
The Canadian Broadcasting Corporation (CBC) is created. It brings radio broadcasts, information and entertainment to Canadian listeners across the country.

1939
World War II breaks out in Europe. Hundreds of thousands of Canadians and Newfoundlanders take part in the conflict.

1949
Newfoundland is the last province to join Canada. It follows Manitoba in 1870, British Columbia in 1871, Prince Edward Island in 1873 and Alberta and Saskatchewan in 1905. The country becomes the size it is today.

British Columbia

Mountains and sea

British Columbia is Canada's westernmost province. It is a place of many different landscapes and spectacular scenery. Lush forests of trees that are over 100 years old grow on its western coast. In the eastern part of the province lie the Rocky Mountains. Hardly any trees grow on the higher slopes. Instead, there are mosses, lichens and low shrubs. In the centre of the province are large, fertile valleys, scattered with small desert areas. More than 24 000 lakes, rivers and streams make British Columbia one of the most water-rich areas in Canada.

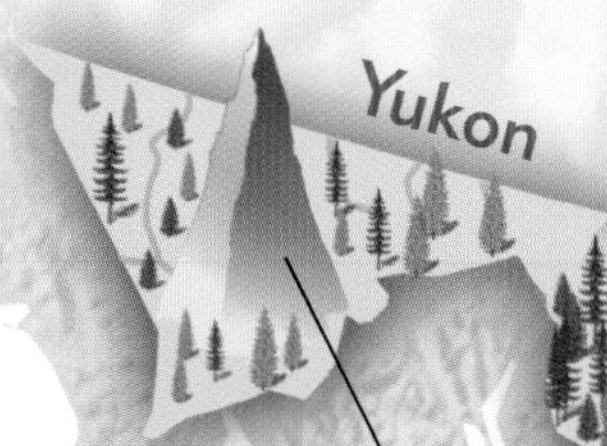

Mount Fairweather is the province's highest mountain peak (4663 metres).

Atlin Lake is the province's largest natural lake.

A forest of giants

The forest near British Columbia's west coast is home to millions of animal and plant ***species***. A lot of rain falls here and the ***climate*** is damp and foggy. This forest has some of the oldest and tallest trees in the world.

Rows of mountains

Three large ***mountain ranges*** cut through British Columbia: the Rocky Mountains, the Columbia Mountains, and the Coast Mountains. British Columbia is Canada's most mountainous region. The Rocky Mountains are the longest mountain range in all of North America.

Origin of the province's name

British Columbia owes its name to the Columbia River, which runs through the south of the province.

Did you know?

The western red cedar of the west coast forest can live to the amazing age of 1000 years!

Queen Charlotte Islands

killer whale

Pacific Ocean

West coast islands

About 6000 islands lie off the western coast of British Columbia. Vancouver Island is the largest in this ***archipelago***. It is five times bigger than Prince Edward Island.

Pacific dogwood

Steller's jay

jade

western red cedar

Treasure in the ground

British Columbia's land is rich in coal. Coal is a fuel that is burned to help produce electricity. The province is also one of the world's biggest ***producers*** of nephrite jade. This stone is usually green, but can range from white to near black. It is a popular choice for jewellery.

Fossils in the Rockies

The Burgess Shale is an area of mud and clay that was discovered in the Rocky Mountains in 1909. It contains tens of thousands of ***fossils***. They are the remains of soft-bodied marine animals that lived 545 million years ago. The Burgess Shale is one of the most important fossil sites in the world.

The **Fraser River** is the longest river in the province (1368 kilometres).

The **Adams River** hosts the greatest inland gathering of sockeye salmon in the world.

Della Falls is the highest waterfall in Canada (440 metres).

A bridge to the world

British Columbia is home to 4 million people, the third-highest population in Canada next to Ontario and Quebec. Half of these people live in the Vancouver area. The province has a wonderful variety of ***cultures*** that include Native peoples like the Gitksan, Nisga'a and Haida, and newcomers from around the world. Its ***economy*** is based on the natural ***resources*** found in its forests and rivers, and in the Pacific Ocean at its western edge. Many British Columbians make their living in the lumber and fishing ***industries***.

Important industries

The forest ***industry*** is the biggest business in British Columbia. Turning wood into paper and construction materials gives jobs to many people in the province. Tourism is the second-biggest business. Every year, the province attracts thousands of visitors. They come to ski, to visit gardens and museums, or just to enjoy the scenery.

The Queen Charlotte Islands

For more than 200 years, the Haida people put up tall totem poles on these islands. According to Haida custom, the animals they carved in the wood served as family crests.

Many faces, many languages

Every year, tens of thousands of people from other parts of Canada and all over the world come to live in British Columbia. Many are from Asia, and bring their own customs and traditions with them. All these newcomers make British Columbia a colourful and interesting place to live.

Pacific Ocean

Do you have your ticket?

West of British Columbia are the Pacific Ocean and Asia. The province is like a bridge connecting Canada to other parts of the world. To connect the province's islands to the mainland, BC Ferries runs one of the biggest fleets of ferry boats in the world. The largest of them carries up to 2100 people and 470 vehicles at a time.

British Columbia's motto
Unlimited splendour

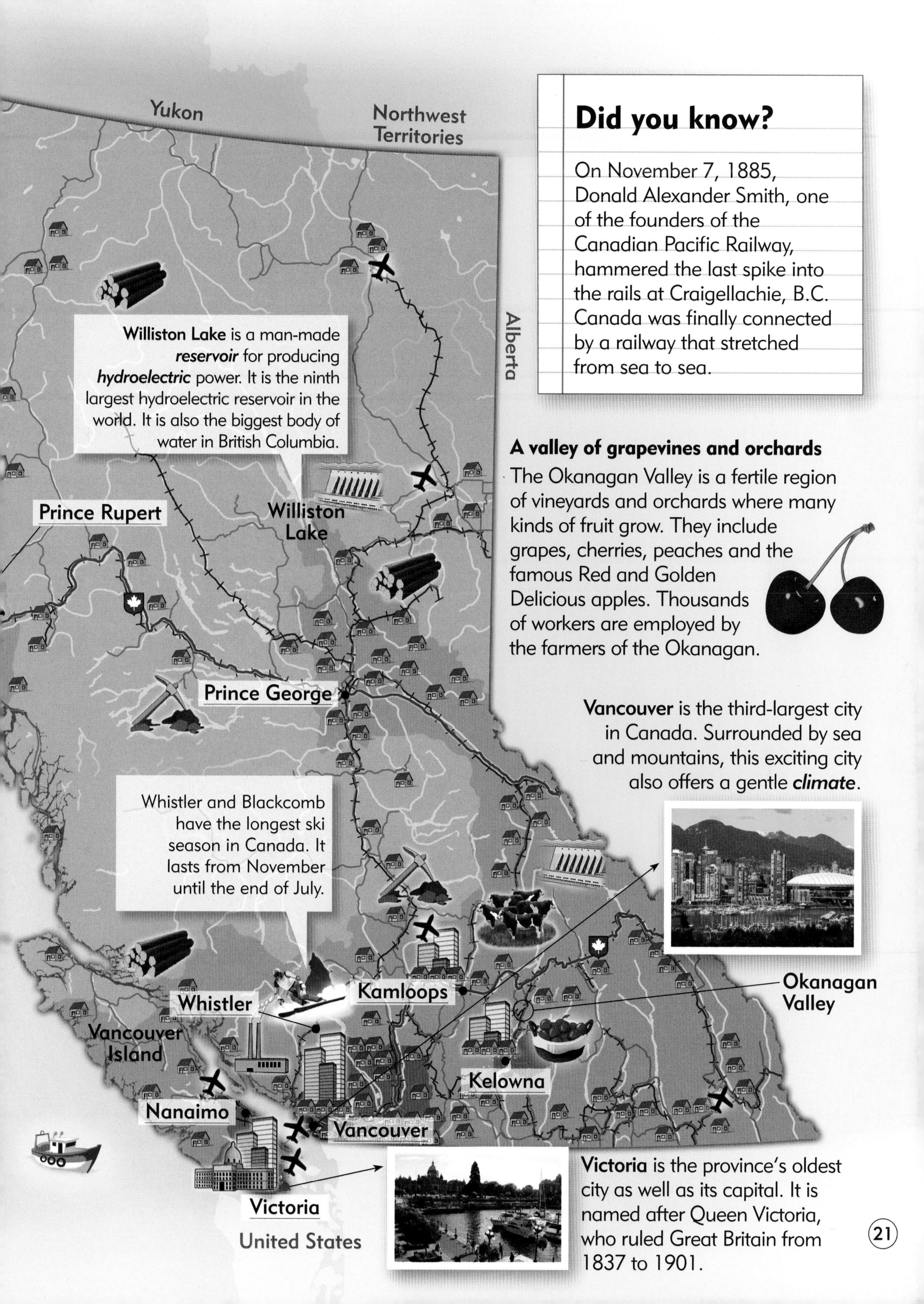

Did you know?

On November 7, 1885, Donald Alexander Smith, one of the founders of the Canadian Pacific Railway, hammered the last spike into the rails at Craigellachie, B.C. Canada was finally connected by a railway that stretched from sea to sea.

A valley of grapevines and orchards

The Okanagan Valley is a fertile region of vineyards and orchards where many kinds of fruit grow. They include grapes, cherries, peaches and the famous Red and Golden Delicious apples. Thousands of workers are employed by the farmers of the Okanagan.

Vancouver is the third-largest city in Canada. Surrounded by sea and mountains, this exciting city also offers a gentle ***climate***.

Victoria is the province's oldest city as well as its capital. It is named after Queen Victoria, who ruled Great Britain from 1837 to 1901.

Alberta

Nature's riches

Alberta is the fourth-largest province in Canada. Along with Saskatchewan and Manitoba, it is part of a large area called the Canadian prairies. This region is known for its farmland and its pastures, where cattle are raised for meat.
The prairies lie in the southern part of the province. They are surrounded by hills, valleys and more than 800 lakes and rivers. The northern half of Alberta is covered in forest. The Rocky Mountains rise in the west, offering a breathtaking landscape.

A "buffalo jump"
The Native peoples of the Alberta plains hunted buffalo, or bison, for more than 5500 years. One method they used was to drive the enormous animals over the edge of a cliff. Today, there are bison bones piled up to 11 metres deep below these cliffs.

Origin of the province's name
The province of Alberta was named after Princess Louise Caroline Alberta. She was the fourth daughter of Queen Victoria.

Snow-eating winds
Chinooks are strong, hot, dry winds that blow out of the Rocky Mountains. In winter, they can melt up to 30 centimetres of snow in just one hour. In the language of the Blackfoot people, chinook means "snow-eater."

Mount Columbia is the tallest mountain in Alberta (3747 metres).

Did you know?

Alberta is the only province in Canada where there are no rats. Since 1950, the province has practised very strict controls to prevent this unwanted animal from invading its territory.

wild rose

petrified wood

great horned owl

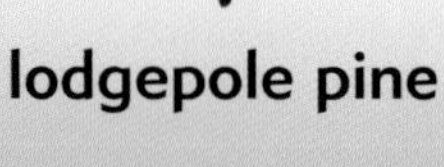

lodgepole pine

Alberta's black gold

The land in Alberta is rich in petroleum, coal and natural gas. These fuels are a precious source of energy. They are used for heating, to produce electricity and to run motorized vehicles.

Breathtaking beauty

There are almost 530 parks and protected areas in Alberta. Banff National Park was the first national park created in Canada. Its spectacular scenery features mountain wilderness, glaciers and deep canyons. Moraine Lake and Lake Louise are the most photographed lakes in the world.

Moraine Lake

Alberta, Canadian capital of the dinosaur

Dinosaur Provincial Park, in Red Deer River Valley, contains the largest deposit of dinosaur bones ever found in the world. Thirty-five *species* of dinosaurs, going back some 75 million years, have been counted here.

Where the gold is black

Alberta has more than 3 million inhabitants. The Native peoples came to this area thousands of years ago. Much later they were joined by ***immigrants*** from Germany, Ukraine and the Scandinavian countries, among others. Farming and raising cattle were Alberta's most important ***industries*** for a long time. After oil was discovered in 1947, however, many people found jobs in the cities. Today, four out of five Albertans live in cities. More than half of them are in Edmonton and Calgary.

Canada's greatest buried treasure

Oil sands are a mixture of sand, water and bitumen (a black substance that looks like molasses). Once the bitumen is separated from the sand, it is transformed into petroleum. Alberta's oil sands deposits are large enough to supply Canada with petroleum for more than 100 years!

Meat, meat, meat!

Nearly one-third of all Canadian beef comes from Alberta. The province has more than 2 million cows and steers. Plains bison are also raised for their meat, and sheep are raised for meat as well as wool.

Jasper is a beautiful town in the Rockies that attracts millions of tourists each year.

The rodeo experience

The Calgary Stampede is one of the biggest outdoor shows in the world. Many farm products and crafts are on display. Cowboys take part in rodeos, where they ride chuckwagons, bucking broncos and Brahma bulls.

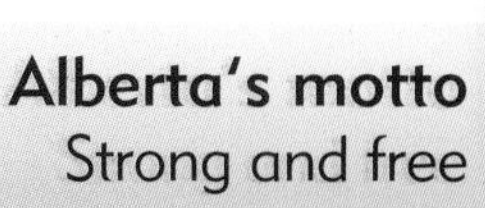

Alberta's motto
Strong and free

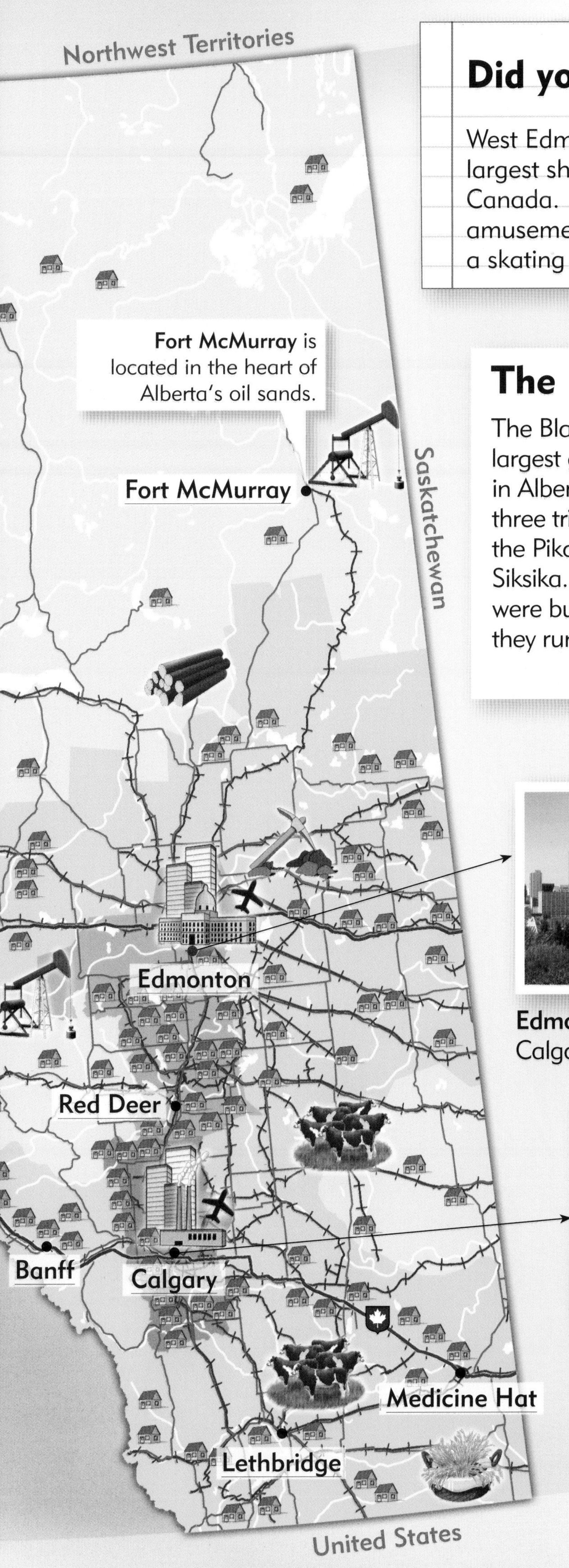

Did you know?

West Edmonton Mall is the largest shopping centre in Canada. It has 800 stores, amusement parks and even a skating rink!

The Blackfoot of Alberta

The Blackfoot Nation is the largest group of Native peoples in Alberta. It is made up of three tribes: the Kainai (Blood), the Pikanii (Peigan) and the Siksika. Long ago, the Blackfoot were buffalo hunters. Today, they run farms and raise cattle.

Edmonton is the capital of Alberta. It and Calgary are the largest cities in the province.

Bustling **Calgary** is home to the Saddledome and the famous Calgary Stampede.

Saskatchewan

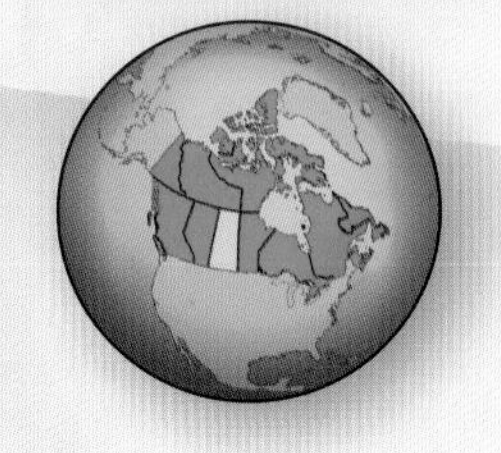

Canada's breadbasket

Saskatchewan is located in the heart of the Canadian prairies, between Alberta and Manitoba. Its oblong shape is the result of boundaries created by humans, not nature. The northern section of the province is filled with forests, ***marshes***, lakes, ponds and rivers. In the southern part, the land is mostly flat, broken here and there by hills and rivers. This region's farmland produces a lot of grain, so Saskatchewan is known as "Canada's breadbasket."

Lake Athabasca

Lake Athabasca is the province's biggest lake.

Natural land sculptures
The dunes in Athabasca Sand Dunes Wilderness Provincial Park rise as high as 30 metres — as tall as a 10-storey building! These land features, which have been sculpted by the wind, are among the northernmost sand dunes in the world.

Alberta

jack pine

North Saskatchewan River

Lloydminster

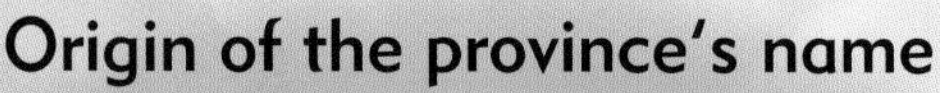

Origin of the province's name
The province takes its name from the Saskatchewan River. The Cree called it *kisiskatchewani sipi*, which means "swift-flowing river."

Overlooking the prairies
Cypress Hills Interprovincial Park is mostly covered in forests of lodgepole pine. Its name comes from early explorers who confused the trees with cypress trees. The area's rolling hills are a contrast to the flatness of the surrounding plains. This is the highest point of land between the Rocky Mountains and Labrador.

The **North and South Saskatchewan rivers** begin in the Rocky Mountains. They meet in Saskatchewan and end in Manitoba after travelling more than 1000 kilometres each.

South Saskatchewan River

The **Cypress Hills** are Saskatchewan's highest point (1392 metres).

lodgepole pine

white birch

sharp-tailed grouse

western red lily

potash

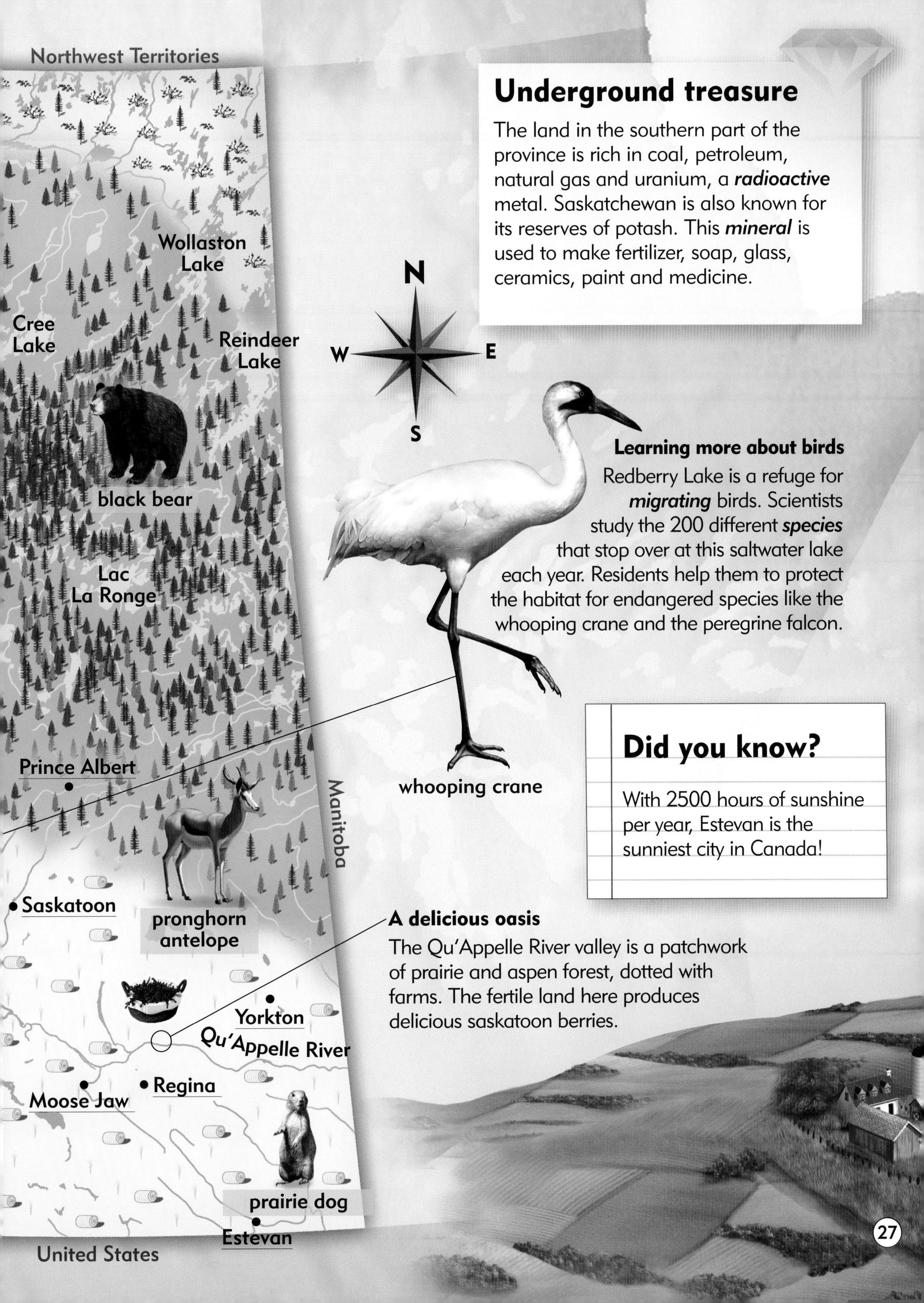

Underground treasure

The land in the southern part of the province is rich in coal, petroleum, natural gas and uranium, a ***radioactive*** metal. Saskatchewan is also known for its reserves of potash. This ***mineral*** is used to make fertilizer, soap, glass, ceramics, paint and medicine.

Learning more about birds

Redberry Lake is a refuge for ***migrating*** birds. Scientists study the 200 different ***species*** that stop over at this saltwater lake each year. Residents help them to protect the habitat for endangered species like the whooping crane and the peregrine falcon.

Did you know?

With 2500 hours of sunshine per year, Estevan is the sunniest city in Canada!

A delicious oasis

The Qu'Appelle River valley is a patchwork of prairie and aspen forest, dotted with farms. The fertile land here produces delicious saskatoon berries.

Western traditions

Saskatchewan has almost 1 million inhabitants. It is the only province where more than half the population are first- or second-generation Canadians. All these people of different origins help make a rich cultural diversity that is the basis of the province's motto: "From many peoples, strength." The province's ***economy*** rests in large part on farming, but its residents also have jobs in the mining and petroleum ***industries***, construction and tourism. In the summertime, the people of Saskatchewan renew their Western traditions, dressing up as pioneers and participating in ***agricultural*** fairs.

Did you know?

Saskatchewan is the only province in Canada that does not use Daylight Saving Time in summer.

Cowboys

Saskatchewan's ranchers are proud of their Western cowboy traditions — and of their horses. These animals play an important part in the lives of the ranchers, who herd their cattle on horseback.

Canada's breadbasket

Saskatchewan is the largest ***producer*** of wheat in the country. More than half of the wheat grown in Canada comes from this province. Other kinds of grain are harvested in Saskatchewan, too, including barley, oats and canola, which is used to make oil and margarine.

Working together for the common good

In 1924, several farming families got together to form the Saskatchewan Wheat Pool. It was one of the first co-operatives in the province. This association made it possible for the farmers to warehouse their grain, sell it in larger quantities and earn more money.

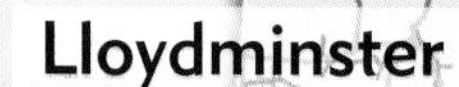

Northwest Territories

The RCMP Training Academy

The Royal Canadian Mounted Police Academy is located in Regina. Its cadets go through strict police training to become officers who are models of discipline and respect. The Mounties' role is to protect Canada's citizens and to ensure that they respect the country's laws.

The colours of Ukraine

A little over a century ago, a wave of 170 000 Ukrainians came to Canada. Many of them settled in Saskatchewan. The traditions of the Ukrainian people are still alive today. They are expressed in art, dancing, opera and theatre.

Prince Albert is located almost exactly in the centre of the province.

Manitoba

Prince Albert

Saskatoon is the largest city in the province. It is known as the "City of Bridges." Seven of them span the South Saskatchewan River, which divides Saskatoon in two.

Moose Jaw

Regina

Regina is the capital of Saskatchewan. It is a city of parks and shaded streets in the middle of sunny prairies.

Under the streets of **Moose Jaw** are secret tunnels dug by Chinese workers in the early 1900s.

Estevan

United States

Saskatchewan's motto
From many peoples, strength

Manitoba

The centre of Canada

Manitoba is located in the heart of Canada. It is as far away from British Columbia in the west as it is from the Atlantic provinces in the east. The southern part includes a fertile triangle of land for farming and for raising animals. The central part of the province has many large lakes with long, sandy beaches. In the north, there are dense forests of ***conifers*** that gradually give way to dry tundra. Large rivers cross this region before flowing into Hudson Bay.

N
W
E
S

Saskatchewan

balsam fir

Manitoba's lakes

Manitoba has more than 100 000 lakes. The largest of them are Winnipeg, Manitoba and Winnipegosis. Most of the northern pike, trout and walleye-pickerel caught in the province come from here.

Origin of the province's name
The province is named after Lake Manitoba. "Manitoba" may have come from the Cree *manito-wapow*, or "the strait where the spirit lives," referring to the Lake Manitoba Narrows.

• Flin Flon

Saskatchewan River

Lake Winnipegosis

Protecting a forest
Riding Mountain National Park is made up of hills and valleys dotted with ***marshes***. Rising suddenly in the middle of the park is Riding Mountain. A vast forest of white spruce grows at the foot of its steep slopes. Endangered ***species***, like the cougar, are being studied in this park.

Baldy Mountain
is the highest mountain in Manitoba (832 metres).

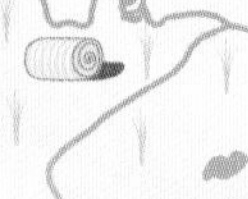

Brandon •

white spruce

great gray owl

prairie crocus

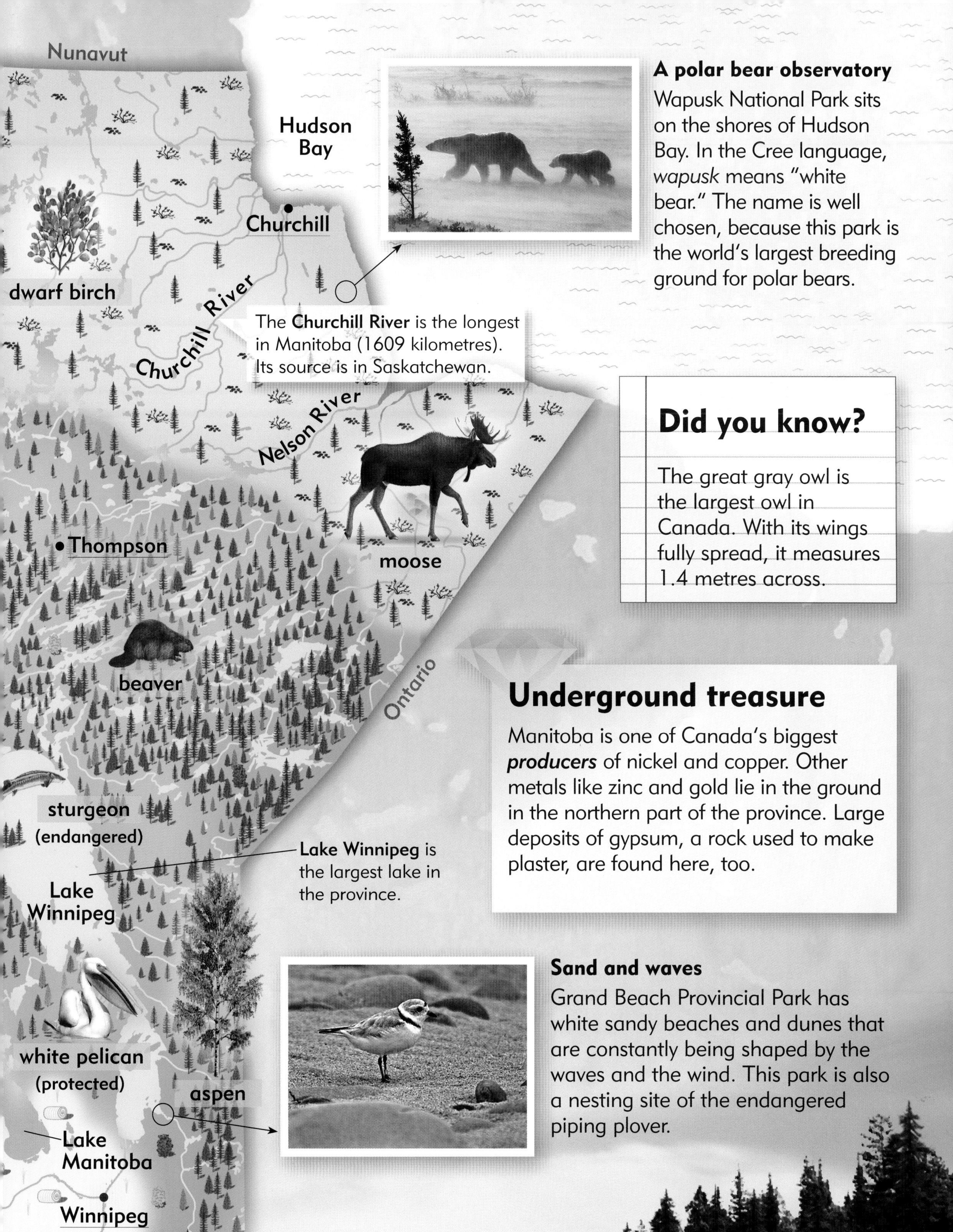

A polar bear observatory

Wapusk National Park sits on the shores of Hudson Bay. In the Cree language, *wapusk* means "white bear." The name is well chosen, because this park is the world's largest breeding ground for polar bears.

Did you know?

The great gray owl is the largest owl in Canada. With its wings fully spread, it measures 1.4 metres across.

Underground treasure

Manitoba is one of Canada's biggest ***producers*** of nickel and copper. Other metals like zinc and gold lie in the ground in the northern part of the province. Large deposits of gypsum, a rock used to make plaster, are found here, too.

Sand and waves

Grand Beach Provincial Park has white sandy beaches and dunes that are constantly being shaped by the waves and the wind. This park is also a nesting site of the endangered piping plover.

At the crossroads

More than 1 150 000 people live in Manitoba. Of these, 700 000 are in the Winnipeg area. Many of those outside the cities are farmers, growing crops like wheat, flax and canola, and raising hogs. The province is known for ***industries*** that process foods, transform metals and manufacture clothes. Because of its central location in Canada, Manitoba is well-placed for transporting merchandise to all parts of the country. The province has a rich ***culture***, developed from a mix of Native Ojibwa, Assiniboine and Cree and the many ***immigrants*** from the United Kingdom, France, Germany and Ukraine.

The Metis, a proud people

The Metis are the descendants of Native peoples and Europeans who intermingled during the 17th, 18th and 19th centuries. Louis Riel, an important 19th-century Metis leader, is considered to be the father of Manitoba.

Flin Flon is a mining centre of more than 6000 inhabitants. Zinc and copper are produced here.

Saskatchewan

Flin Flon

A symbol of pride

The Golden Boy is Manitoba's most famous landmark. This 1650 kilogram statue of a young man holding a torch and a sheaf of wheat stands on top of the Legislative Building in Winnipeg.

Brandon is the second-largest city in the province.

Brandon

Manitoba's motto
Glorious and free

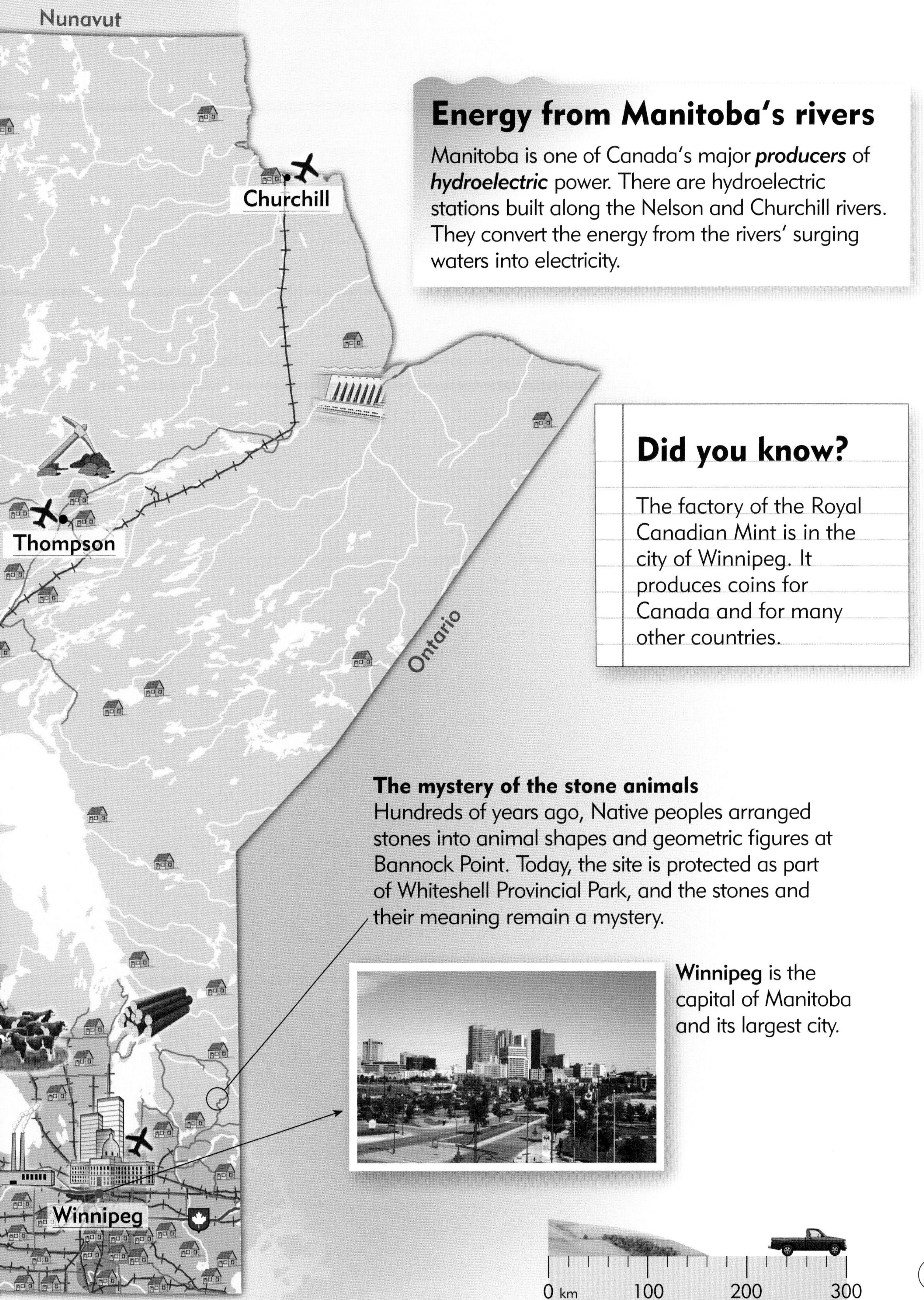

Energy from Manitoba's rivers

Manitoba is one of Canada's major ***producers*** of ***hydroelectric*** power. There are hydroelectric stations built along the Nelson and Churchill rivers. They convert the energy from the rivers' surging waters into electricity.

Did you know?

The factory of the Royal Canadian Mint is in the city of Winnipeg. It produces coins for Canada and for many other countries.

The mystery of the stone animals
Hundreds of years ago, Native peoples arranged stones into animal shapes and geometric figures at Bannock Point. Today, the site is protected as part of Whiteshell Provincial Park, and the stones and their meaning remain a mystery.

Winnipeg is the capital of Manitoba and its largest city.

Ontario

A living landscape

Ontario is Canada's second-largest province. Its 250 000 lakes and countless rivers, vast forests, meadows and wetlands provide a variety of habitats for many kinds of animals. Ontario's varied landscapes are also appreciated by outdoor enthusiasts who fish, hunt, canoe, ski and camp in its more than 300 provincial parks.

Lake Superior is the largest freshwater lake in the world.

Origin of the province's name
The name "Ontario" may be a variation of the Iroquoian word *onitariio*, or "beautiful water."

Did you know?

Manitoulin Island is the largest island in any freshwater lake in the world. It lies in Lake Huron, and is five times bigger than the island of Montreal in Quebec.

The Great Lakes

Lakes Superior, Michigan, Huron, Erie and Ontario form the largest ***reservoir*** of fresh water in the world. The Ontario-United States border runs through four of the Great Lakes, dividing them almost equally in two. Lake Michigan lies entirely on the American side of the border.

white trillium

amethyst

common loon

eastern white pine

Hudson Bay

N
E
S
W

Large forests

Two-thirds of Ontario is covered with forests. This natural ***resource*** is important to the Canadian wood ***industry***. The trees supply paper as well as construction materials.

James Bay

Albany River

Moosonee

Moose River

Quebec

red-tailed hawk

Underground riches

The bedrock of Ontario is rich in metals like silver, zinc, copper, gold and nickel. Ontario is the world's second-largest ***producer*** of nickel. This silver-white metal is used to make batteries and coins.

Timmins

white-tailed deer

The **Ottawa River** (1130 kilometres) marks the boundary between Quebec and Ontario.

Ishpatina Ridge is Ontario's tallest summit (693 metres).

Ottawa River

Sudbury

French River

Ottawa

Cornwall

Manitoulin Island

Lake Michigan

Lake Huron

walleye

red oak

Kingston

Oshawa

Lake Ontario

Toronto

Point Pelee is the southernmost point in Canada. More than 370 ***species*** of birds live in this national park. It is an important ***migratory flyway*** for birds and for the monarch butterfly, and warm enough for the eastern prickly pear cactus, an endangered species.

coyote

St. Catharines-Niagara

Hamilton

Kitchener

Windsor

Lake Erie

London

Spectacular waterfalls

Niagara Falls stretches almost a kilometre across. Every minute, 155 million litres of water, equal to 50 Olympic-size pools, spill over the edge and fall 17 storeys!

The heart of Canada

There are 12 million people in Ontario, more than in any other province. One-third of Canadians live here, mostly in the Great Lakes region. Here a wealth of cities and ***industries*** make it an important economic centre. Half of Canada's ***immigrants*** settle in Ontario. Many come from Europe, Asia and the Caribbean. Native peoples add to the mix of ***cultures***. The province is also an important centre for the arts, with many museums, galleries and theatres.

Manitoba

United States

Thunder Bay

Thunder Bay is the largest city in northern Ontario.

The best farmland in the country

The best farmland in Canada is found in southern Ontario. Grain, potatoes, soybeans and many kinds of vegetables and fruit, including peaches, apples and grapes, are grown here.

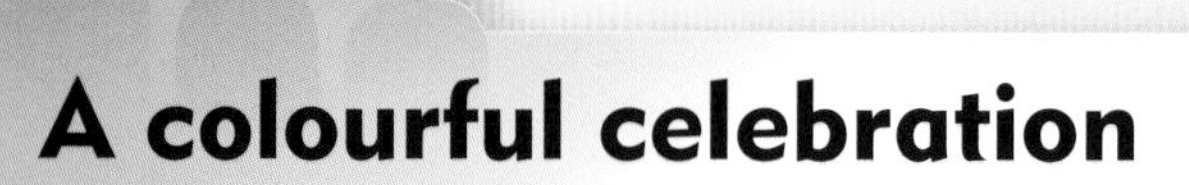

A colourful celebration

Cultures from all corners of the world thrive in Ontario. The rich blend of customs is displayed in a multitude of celebrations. Caribana, an annual Caribbean festival in Toronto, features storytelling, music, costumes and dancing.

Ontario's motto
Loyal she began, loyal she remains

Did you know?

Highway 401, which connects the cities of Windsor and Cornwall in Ontario, is 820 kilometres long. With more than 400 000 vehicles travelling on it every day, the 401 is one of the busiest roads in the world!

Important industries

Ontario is Canada's manufacturing leader and produces almost 60% of all exported manufactured goods, like building materials and electronic products. Automobile manufacturing is a big part of Ontario's ***economy***. More than 140 000 Ontarians work in this ***industry***. They build cars, vans, trucks, buses and military vehicles.

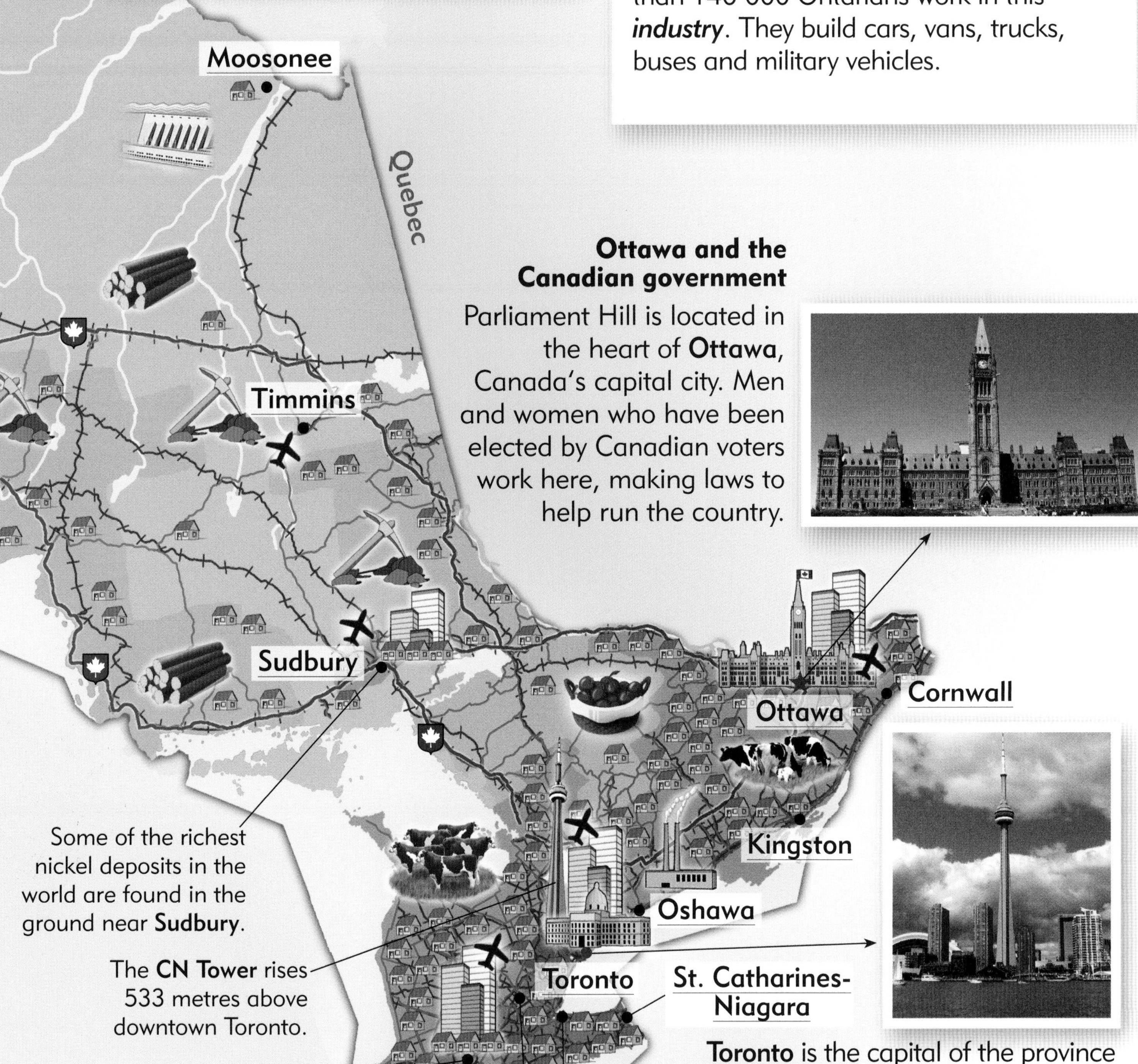

Ottawa and the Canadian government

Parliament Hill is located in the heart of **Ottawa**, Canada's capital city. Men and women who have been elected by Canadian voters work here, making laws to help run the country.

Some of the richest nickel deposits in the world are found in the ground near **Sudbury**.

The **CN Tower** rises 533 metres above downtown Toronto.

Toronto is the capital of the province and the largest city in Canada. More than 70 languages are spoken here, including English, French, Chinese, Italian and German.

Quebec

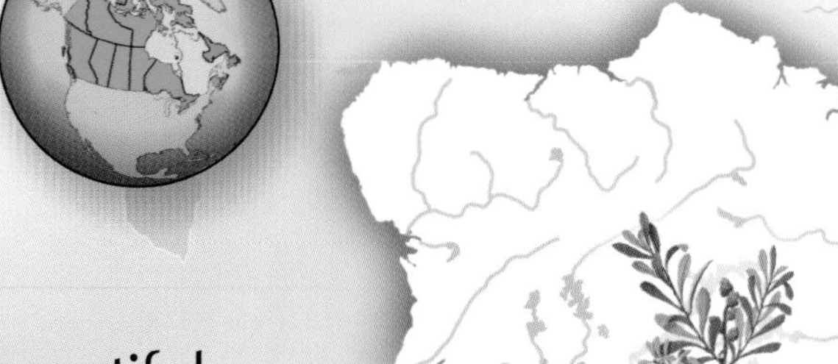

A beautiful province

Quebec is the largest Canadian province. Its beautiful landscapes have earned it the nickname "La belle province." Old mountains, wrinkled and rounded, cross the southern part of Quebec from west to east. The St. Lawrence River also runs through the south and flows into the Atlantic Ocean. The land along the river is well suited to farming. North of the St. Lawrence River is a mountainous region called the Laurentians. The rest of this vast territory is flat and covered in dense forest. Quebec has more than 130 000 rivers and 1 million lakes.

Forests as far as the eye can see!

Almost half of Quebec is covered in forest. These leafy trees and ***conifers*** are very important to the province. Their wood is used to make paper, cardboard and construction materials.

Origin of the province's name

The province of Quebec takes its name from the Algonquin word *kebec*, which means "where the river narrows." It refers to the narrowing of the St. Lawrence River near Quebec City.

Did you know?

The cold waters of the Saguenay ***fjord*** are rich in fish, shrimp, squid and sea worms — the favourite foods of the beluga whale. The beluga's name comes from the Russian word *belyi*, meaning "white."

bog myrtle

Hudson Bay

Great Whale River

La Grande River

river otter

James Bay

Ontario

snowshoe hare

Ottawa River

yellow birch

wild iris

snowy owl

Underground treasure

Beneath the surface, Quebec is rich in ***minerals*** like gold, silver, copper, zinc and iron. The largest deposit of asbestos in Canada is found in the town of Asbestos. This fibre is used to make some automotive parts as well as boats.

A marine bird wonderland

The Magdalen Islands ***archipelago*** is a chain of about a dozen islands in the Gulf of St. Lawrence. This area has beautiful beaches and golden sand dunes. Thousands of birds make their nests near the islands' majestic red cliffs.

Enchanting scenery

La Mauricie National Park is located in the heart of the Laurentian Mountains. Many streams and pretty waterfalls run through its forest-covered hills. The park is an ideal location for outdoor activities.

A unique province

More than 7 million people live in Quebec. It is the province with the second-highest population in Canada. The majority of Quebecers are ***francophone***, which makes this province unique. Quebec's original inhabitants include the Cree, Innu and Mi'kmaq. Inuit live in the northernmost regions. Many ***immigrants*** have come from Europe, Africa, Latin America and Asia. The province's ***economy*** is based on farming, mining, forestry and ***hydroelectric*** power. Quebec also specializes in space science, health and telecommunications.

Did you know?

A Quebecer named Joseph-Armand Bombardier introduced his invention, the Ski-Dog, in 1959. He designed this first snowmobile to allow people to travel easily on snow. It became known as the Ski-Doo.

Food from the farm

Quebec is the biggest dairy ***producer*** in Canada. The milk from Quebec cows is turned into cheese, yogurt, butter and cream. Quebec's farmers also raise pigs, chicken and cattle for their meat.

Ontario

Do you speak French?

Quebec is the only province in Canada where French is the most common language. Four out of five Quebecers speak French at home, at school and in the workplace. People in Quebec are very proud of their roots.

Quebec's motto
"Je me souviens" (I remember)

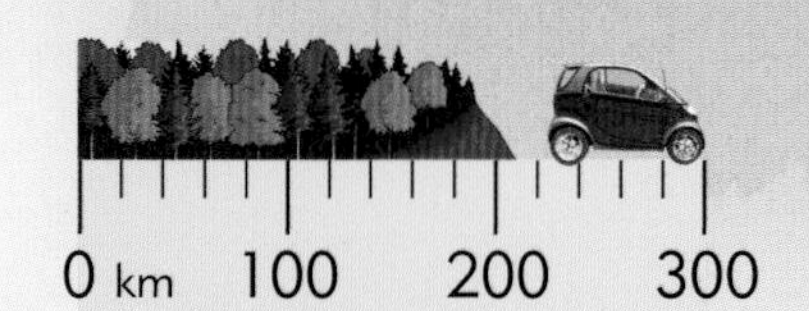

Energy from water

Quebec is the largest ***producer*** of ***hydroelectric*** power in Canada. It supplies all the electricity needed for the people of the province. The extra electricity is sold to neighbouring provinces and parts of the United States.

Springtime is sweet!
Quebec is the largest ***producer*** of maple syrup and maple sugar in the world. Every spring, maple syrup producers collect the sap from maple trees and turn it into syrup. Native peoples introduced the first French settlers to this sweet treat.

The name "Gaspé" comes from the Mi'kmaq word *Gespeg*, meaning "land's end."

Quebec City is the capital as well as the oldest city in the province. It is the only city in Canada with its original ***fortifications***.

Montreal is the largest city in Quebec. It is also the second-largest French-speaking city in the world.

New Brunswick

A gateway to the Maritimes

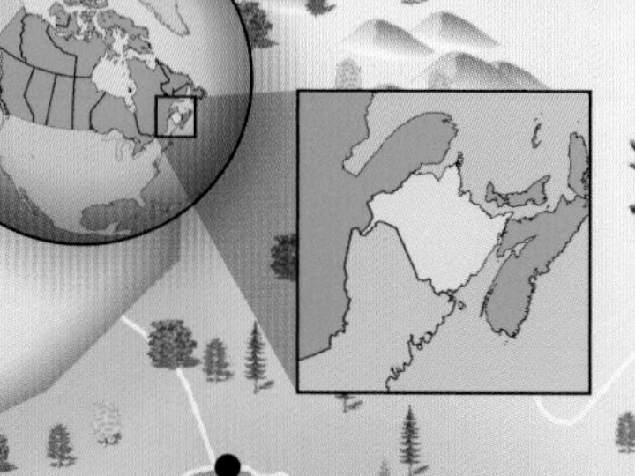

The three provinces bordering on the Atlantic Ocean are called the Maritime provinces. They are New Brunswick, Nova Scotia and Prince Edward Island. New Brunswick is the gateway to the Maritimes and the largest of the three provinces. This region offers a variety of landscapes. In the north lie the mountains of the Appalachian range. In the south, there are rolling hills covered in forest. The province's coast has sandy beaches, warm waters and superb landscapes that have been carved by the action of the waves.

Grand Falls is the highest waterfall in the Maritime provinces. The waters of the Saint John River drop from a height of 23 metres — higher than a seven-storey building.

The **Saint John River** is the longest river in New Brunswick (673 kilometres).

Majestic forests

About 85% of New Brunswick is covered in forests. Hundreds of rivers run through them. This beautiful natural environment provides shelter for many kinds of animals.

Origin of the province's name

The province was named in honour of King George III, a ruler of the British Isles who was descended from the House of Brunswick.

Treasures of the earth

The land in New Brunswick is rich in metals like silver, copper, gold and lead, as well as ***minerals*** such as potash and salt. Materials used in construction, including sand, gravel and stone, are also found here.

Did you know?

The oldest shark ***fossil*** was found near the city of Campbellton. The 409-million-year-old creature measured barely 50 centimetres in length.

purple violet

black-capped chickadee

balsam fir

Mount Carleton is the highest peak in the Maritime provinces (820 metres).

Protecting nature

New Brunswick has many parks and natural sites that have been set up to protect the plants and animals living there. The Bouctouche Dune is one of North America's last great sand dunes.

Grand Lake is the largest lake in New Brunswick.

The highest tides in the world

The Bay of Fundy has the highest tides in the world. In some places, the water rises 16 metres in just a few hours. That is the height of a five-storey building!

Grand Manan Island is a paradise for nature lovers, who can observe more than 330 different bird ***species***. The waters surrounding the island attract whales and dolphins.

The land of the Acadians

The first people living in New Brunswick were the native Mi'kmaq and Maliseet. About 400 years ago, they were joined by the French, who became the Acadians. Following them came the English, the Scots and the Irish, as well as ***immigrants*** from other countries. Most of New Brunswick's 730 000 people live in cities and towns along the coast and in the Saint John River Valley. Many of them work in the food, pulp and paper, and forestry ***industries***. Others fish or farm. New Brunswick is the only province in Canada that is officially bilingual. Most people speak English, but one-third of the population is ***francophone***.

Quebec

Edmunston

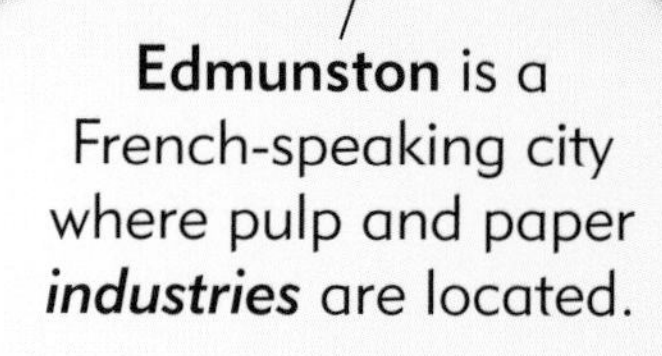

Edmunston is a French-speaking city where pulp and paper ***industries*** are located.

United States

The longest covered bridge in the world is in **Hartland**. It is 390 metres long.

Hartland

Friendly people

Many of New Brunswick's Acadians live in small villages on the Atlantic coast. A friendly and proud people, the Acadians have a colourful ***culture*** in which music, dance and traditional foods play an important part.

Did you know?

A hundred years ago in St. Stephen, the Ganong candy factory produced the world's first wrapped chocolate bar.

St. Stephen

New Brunswick's motto
Hope restored

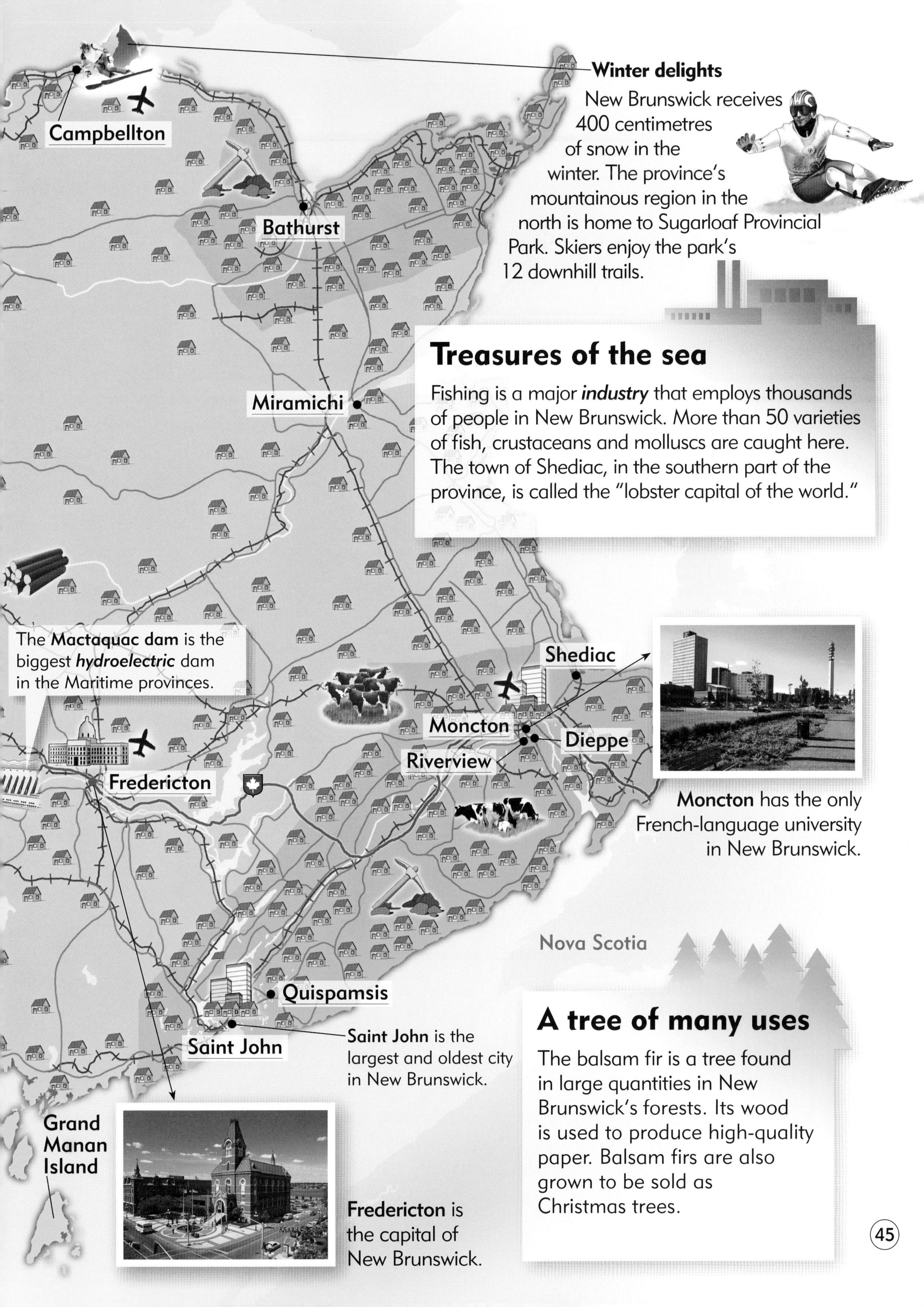

Winter delights

New Brunswick receives 400 centimetres of snow in the winter. The province's mountainous region in the north is home to Sugarloaf Provincial Park. Skiers enjoy the park's 12 downhill trails.

Treasures of the sea

Fishing is a major ***industry*** that employs thousands of people in New Brunswick. More than 50 varieties of fish, crustaceans and molluscs are caught here. The town of Shediac, in the southern part of the province, is called the "lobster capital of the world."

The **Mactaquac dam** is the biggest ***hydroelectric*** dam in the Maritime provinces.

Moncton has the only French-language university in New Brunswick.

Saint John is the largest and oldest city in New Brunswick.

Fredericton is the capital of New Brunswick.

A tree of many uses

The balsam fir is a tree found in large quantities in New Brunswick's forests. Its wood is used to produce high-quality paper. Balsam firs are also grown to be sold as Christmas trees.

Nova Scotia

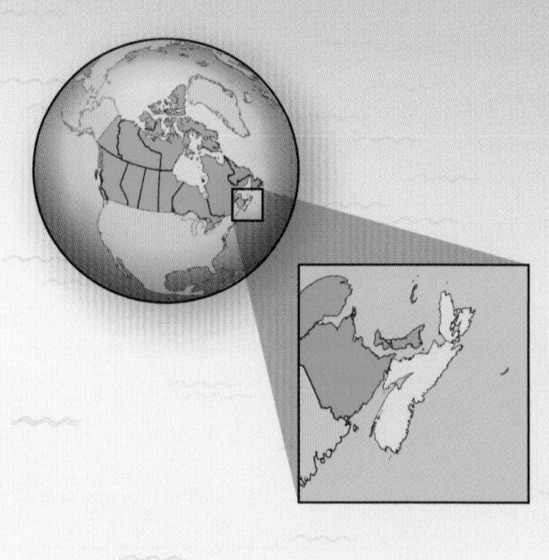

Between land and sea

Nova Scotia is almost an island. It is attached to New Brunswick by a narrow strip of land called the Isthmus of Chicnecto. On the Atlantic Ocean side, the coast forms a lacy band of capes and small bays. Along Northumberland Strait are sandy beaches bathed by warm waters. Nova Scotia also includes more than 870 islands. The largest of them is Cape Breton Island. Its beautiful landscapes are home to a variety of plants and animals. Inland, the province is rocky and hilly.

Nova Scotia has many forests and streams and more than 3000 lakes.

Origin of the province's name
Nova Scotia means "New Scotland" in Latin. The province was named in honour of the first Scottish settlers.

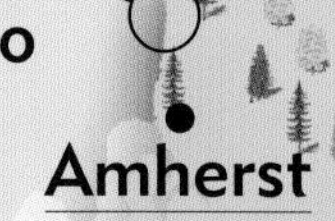

Against the current

Twice a day, a wave travels "backward" up the Salmon River, against the current. This strange phenomenon is caused by powerful tides rising in the Bay of Fundy and overflowing into the river.

The oldest reptile
The oldest known reptile is *Hylonomus lyelli*. This animal lived on Earth 315 million years ago. ***Fossils*** of this prehistoric creature have been found in the hollow stumps of ancient trees in Nova Scotia.

mayflower

osprey

stilbite

red spruce

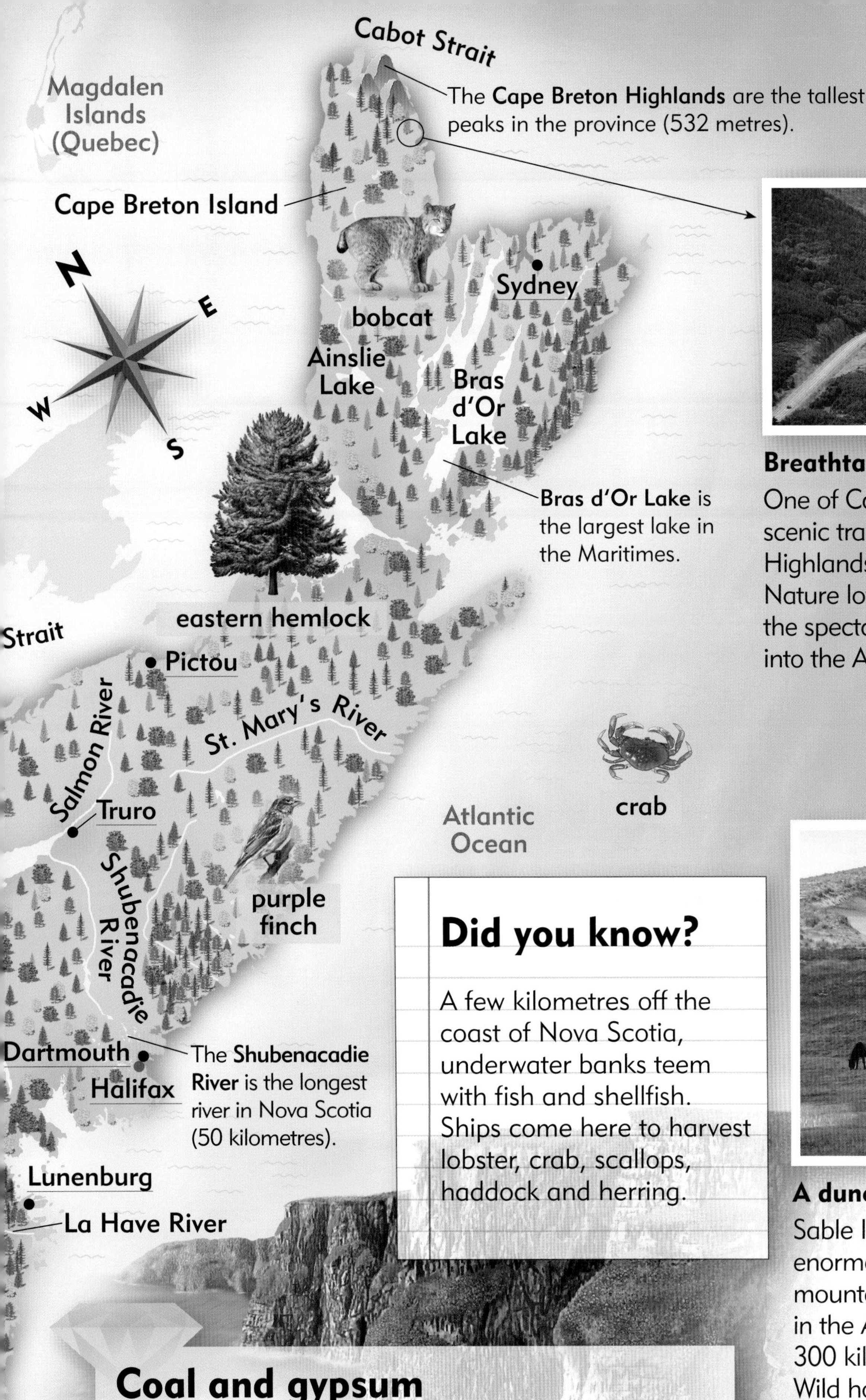

The **Cape Breton Highlands** are the tallest peaks in the province (532 metres).

Bras d'Or Lake is the largest lake in the Maritimes.

The **Shubenacadie River** is the longest river in Nova Scotia (50 kilometres).

Breathtaking landscapes

One of Canada's most beautiful scenic trails is in Cape Breton Highlands National Park. Nature lovers here can admire the spectacular cliffs that plunge into the Atlantic Ocean.

Did you know?

A few kilometres off the coast of Nova Scotia, underwater banks teem with fish and shellfish. Ships come here to harvest lobster, crab, scallops, haddock and herring.

Sable Island

A dune under the ocean

Sable Island is the top of an enormous dune, or sand mountain, that has formed in the Atlantic Ocean 300 kilometres from Halifax. Wild horses have been living here for hundreds of years. The dune is high enough to bury a 13-storey building!

Coal and gypsum

Large coal deposits lie underground in Nova Scotia. This ***combustible*** material is used in electrical power plants. Nova Scotia also supplies most of the gypsum in Canada. Gypsum is a rock used as construction material.

A vibrant history

With more than 900 000 inhabitants, Nova Scotia has the highest population of the Maritime provinces. Most Nova Scotians live in cities along the coast. Many of them work in the forest, mining and tourist ***industries***. Fishing is also an important part of the ***economy***. Cod, haddock, pollock, lobster, scallops and crab are the main catch. Nova Scotia's first inhabitants were the Mi'kmaq. They were joined by ***immigrants*** who sailed from France 400 years ago, the first Europeans to settle in Canada. They were followed by the English, the Scots and the Irish, as well as immigrants from Germany and the Netherlands.

Did you know?

New Brunswick and Prince Edward Island were once part of Nova Scotia. The provinces were separated more than 200 years ago.

Prince Edward Island

Northumberlar

New Brunswick

Amherst is the gateway to Nova Scotia.

Amherst

Bay of Fundy

The most fertile land in the province is the **Annapolis Valley**, which is famous for its delicious apples.

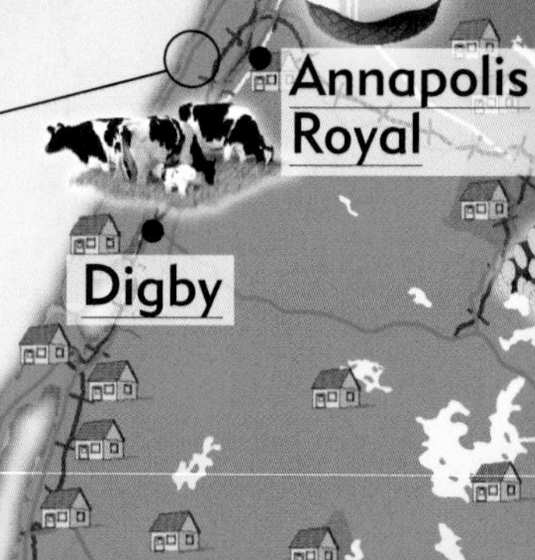

Shelburne

Yarmouth

The cradle of Acadia

The French established a settlement in Canada in 1605 called Port-Royal. It was situated on the shores of the Bay of Fundy, near the present-day town of Annapolis Royal. This area was called Acadie. Many Acadian villages exist in Nova Scotia to this day.

Nova Scotia's motto
One defends and the other conquers

0 km 50 100

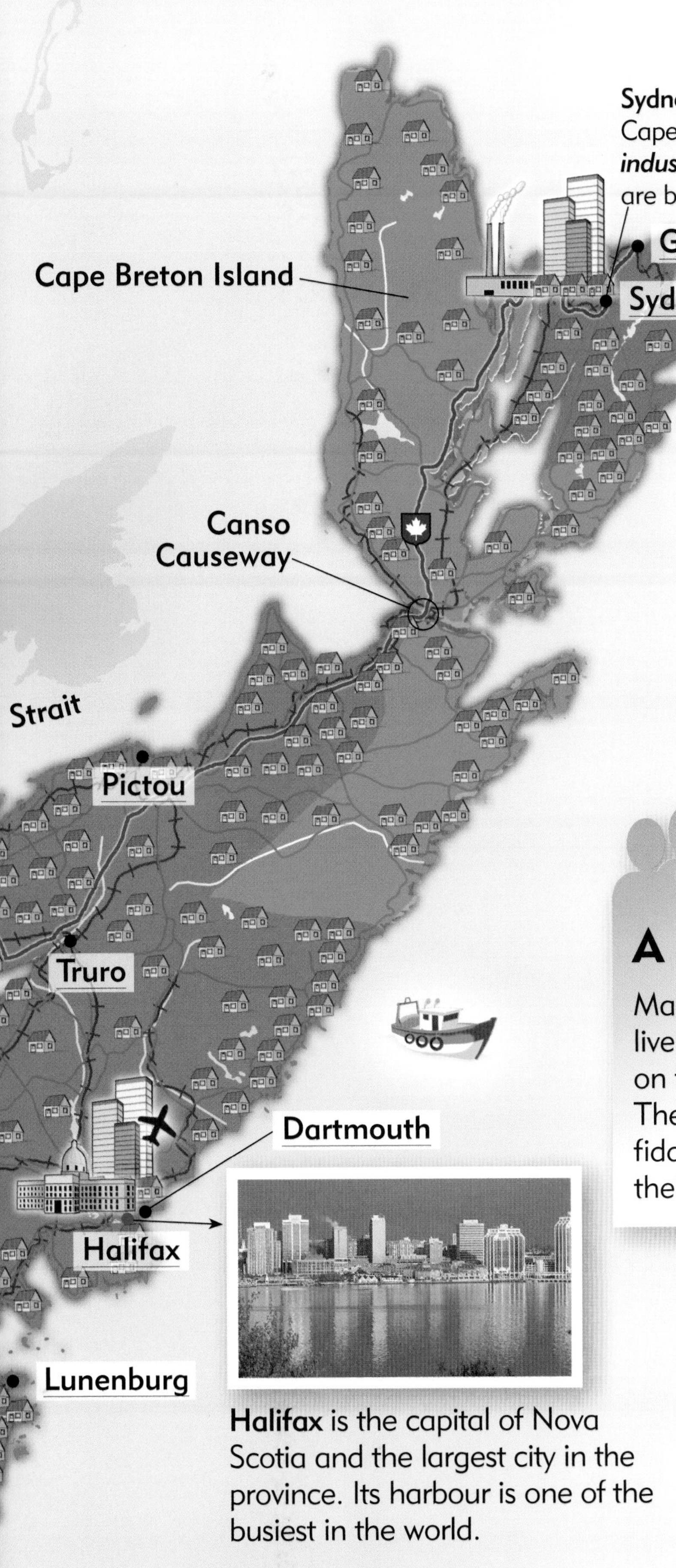

Sydney is the largest city on Cape Breton Island. Many ***industries*** and businesses are based here.

Defending Canada

For a long time the city of Halifax played an important role in the defence of Canada's east coast. The construction of the Halifax Citadel took 28 years and was completed in 1856. It was designed to protect the city in case of attack.

A rich heritage

Many descendants of Scottish ***immigrants*** live in Nova Scotia. Most of them settled on the shores of Northumberland Strait. Their songs and dances, accompanied by fiddles or bagpipes, are a reminder of their origins.

Halifax is the capital of Nova Scotia and the largest city in the province. Its harbour is one of the busiest in the world.

A famous sailing ship

The *Bluenose* was a famous fishing schooner. The 43.6-metre-long boat was built in Lunenburg in 1921. She won nearly every race in which she sailed. Since 1937, she has appeared on Canada's 10-cent coin. Today people admire her replica, the *Bluenose II*.

Prince Edward Island

A green and gentle landscape

Prince Edward Island is the smallest province in Canada. It is separated from New Brunswick and Nova Scotia by the Northumberland Strait. This small island is famous for its beauty and unique charm. It is a landscape of pretty rolling hills in shades of green, yellow and ochre. Bordering this peaceful countryside are majestic red cliffs and the clear blue waters of the Atlantic that surround the province. There are very few lakes and rivers on Prince Edward Island. More than half of the province is covered in forest.

Rusty ground

Prince Edward Island's soil contains iron. When this ***mineral*** comes in contact with oxygen in the air, it oxidizes, or rusts. It is the rusting iron in the earth that gives this island its unique reddish colour.

Origin of the province's name

The province was named after Great Britain's Prince Edward, Duke of Kent, in 1799.

Did you know?

No matter where you are on the island, the ocean is never more than 16 kilometres away.

lady's slipper

red oak

blue jay

A park along the sea

Prince Edward Island National Park stretches along the province's north shore. It is a protected area of red sandstone cliffs, salt ***marshes*** and freshwater ponds where many threatened ***species*** of plants and animals live.

The **Hillsborough River**, named *Mimtugaak* by the Mi'kmaq, is the longest river on the island (45 kilometres).

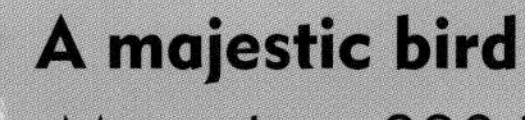

A majestic bird

More than 330 bird ***species*** nest on Prince Edward Island. Among them is the great blue heron. These majestic birds gather in large colonies along the province's shores.

The highest point in the province is in the **Bonshaw Hills** (142 metres).

Beautiful beaches and dunes

The beaches on Prince Edward Island are among the most beautiful in North America. In some places, white sand stretches as far as the eye can see. In other areas, the sand forms dunes that change shape with the passing seasons.

The birthplace of Canada

Although it has only 138 000 inhabitants, Prince Edward Island is the most densely populated province in Canada, thanks to its small size. Most ***islanders*** live in the country. There are many small towns and only two cities. The first residents on the island were the Mi'kmaq. They were joined by settlers from France, part of the ***colony*** called Acadia. Today, one out of 10 residents is of Acadian origin. ***Immigrants*** from England, Ireland and Scotland followed. Today, eight out of 10 islanders come from those roots. Agriculture and fishing employ many people, and tourism is a very important part of the ***economy***. Every year, Prince Edward Island receives about 1 million visitors — nearly 10 times the population of the province!

The birth of a country

Province House is in Charlottetown. Here, in 1864, political delegates met for the first time to discuss the creation of Canada. Because of this historic event, Prince Edward Island is known as the "Birthplace of Confederation."

Tignish

Alberton

Lennox Island

O'Leary

Malpeque

Summerside

Wellington

The **Evangeline Region** is a thriving Acadian ***community*** that is proud of its origins.

Summerside is the second-largest city.

New Brunswick

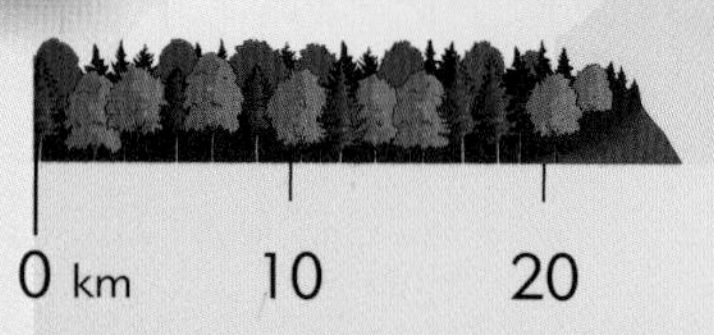

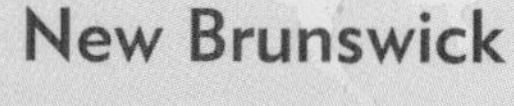

0 km 10 20 30 40 50

A living culture

The Mi'kmaq have been living on Prince Edward Island for 10 000 years. Lennox Island and Scotchfort are two ***communities*** where the Mi'kmaq ***culture*** is alive and well.

Prince Edward Island's motto

The small under the protection of the great

Each year, thousands of people come to the town of **Cavendish** to visit Green Gables, the famous house that inspired Lucy Maud Montgomery to write her novel *Anne of Green Gables*.

Charlottetown is the capital of Prince Edward Island and the province's largest city.

Did you know?

Prince Edward Island was called "Île-Saint-Jean" by the first French ***colonists*** who settled here.

A fertile land

Half of the province is devoted to farming. The reddish soil on the island is ideal for growing potatoes and other vegetables and fruits. Prince Edward Island provides one-third of Canada's potatoes.

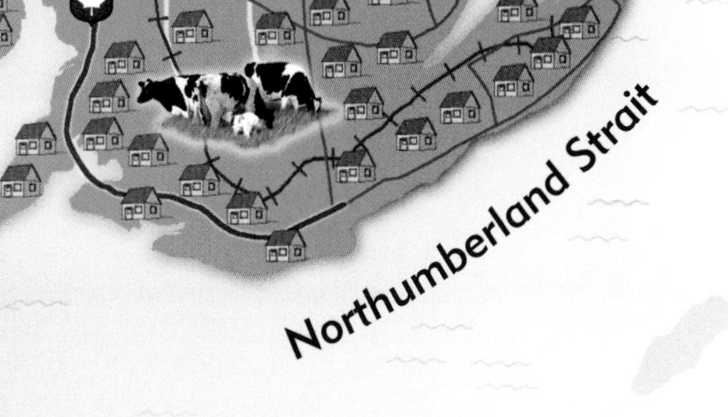

A bridge to the continent

Since 1997, travellers have been able to drive across a 12.9-kilometre bridge that links Prince Edward Island to New Brunswick. The Confederation Bridge is a marvel of engineering. It was designed to withstand ice freeze-ups in the Northumberland Strait.

Nova Scotia

Newfoundland and Labrador

A land of rugged beauty

Newfoundland and Labrador is the easternmost province in Canada. It is made up of two separate regions. Newfoundland is a triangular island that sits in the Atlantic Ocean. Labrador is part of the mainland of Canada. It is bordered by Quebec. Newfoundland's picturesque landscape includes mountains, craggy cliffs and deep ***fjords***. The northern part of Labrador is a huge wilderness area of gigantic mountains without ***vegetation***. Much of Newfoundland and Labrador is covered in dense forest. The forest is a habitat for a wide variety of plants and animals.

Mount Caubvick is the tallest peak in the province (1652 metres). Across the Quebec border, the mountain is called Mount Iberville.

Labrador Sea

N E S W

Labrador's ***mountain ranges*** are among the oldest on the planet.

caribou

balsam fir

The province's largest lake is man-made — the **Smallwood Reservoir** in Labrador.

Smallwood Reservoir

Churchill Falls

Labrador

Labrador City

Wabush

Riches of the earth

Labrador's soil is rich in iron. This greyish-white metal is used to make steel. Nickel, copper and cobalt are mined on the island of Newfoundland.

Origin of Labrador's name
For hundreds of years, Portuguese ships crossed the Atlantic to fish along the coast of Labrador. The name probably comes from the Portuguese *lavrador*, which means "landowner."

The **wild partridgeberry** is a low evergreen shrub. Its tart little fruits make delicious jam.

pitcher plant

Atlantic puffin

labradorite

black spruce

An amazing underwater world

Much of this province's territory is actually underwater! It is called the Grand Banks. The sunken land forms a shallow platform under the ocean. It is more than two and a half times the size of the island of Newfoundland, and is home to an amazing variety of marine life.

Did you know?

The province's caribou herd is one of the largest in the world. More than 700 000 caribou travel through this region.

Floating islands of ice

Every spring, thousands of icebergs break off from glaciers in the North Atlantic and float south along the coast of Labrador and Newfoundland. Only a small fraction of each iceberg is visible. The rest is hidden underwater.

Birds by the millions

Baccalieu Island is home to the largest colony of Leach's storm petrels in the world. Seven million of these seabirds nest here, as well as 150 000 Atlantic puffins.

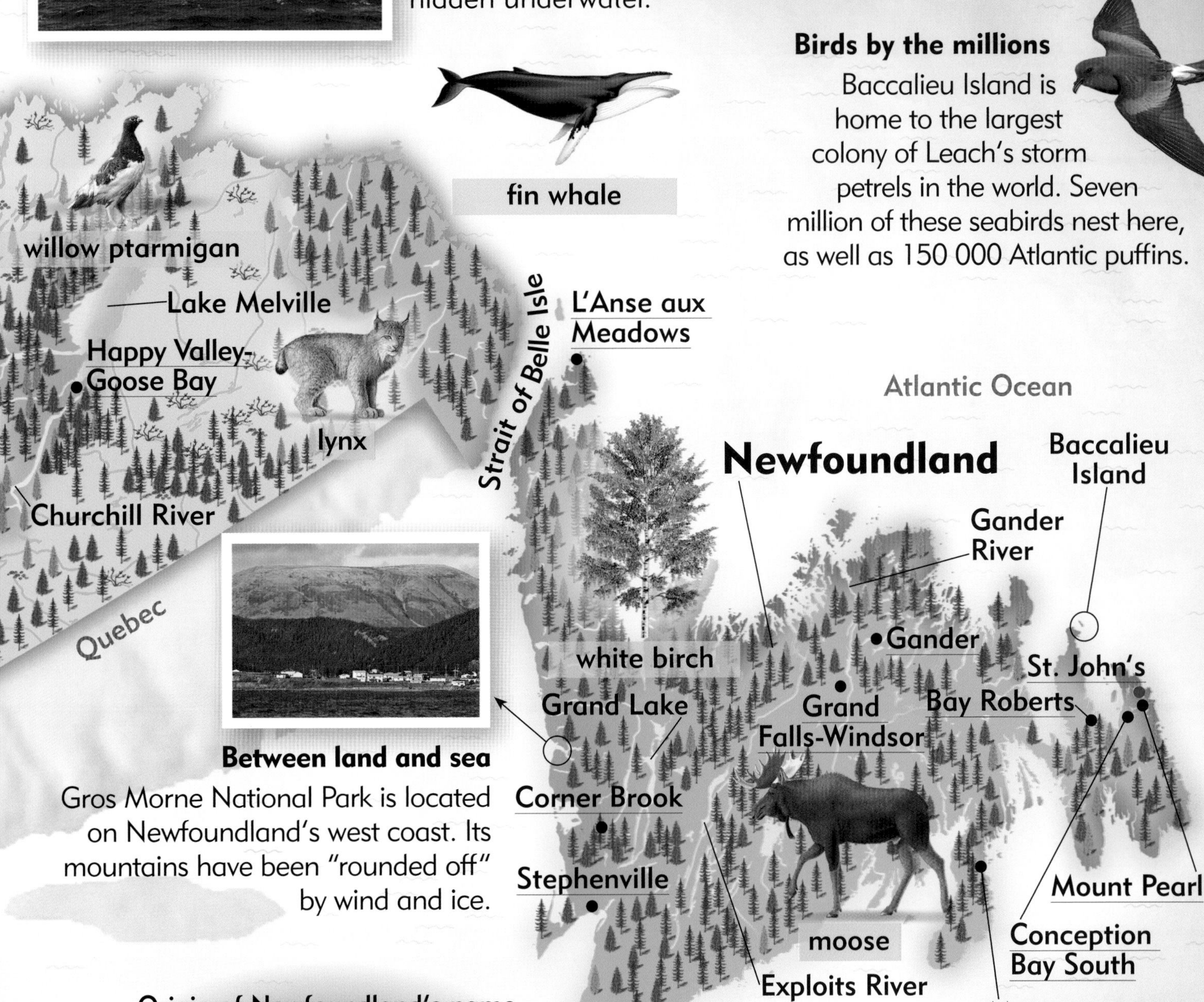

Between land and sea

Gros Morne National Park is located on Newfoundland's west coast. Its mountains have been "rounded off" by wind and ice.

Origin of Newfoundland's name

Italian explorer John Cabot called it a "new found isle," and soon "New Found Launde" was being used in English documents.

Always a friendly welcome

The history of Newfoundland and Labrador is very closely tied to fishing. The province's first inhabitants, the Beothuk, were skilled whale hunters. In turn, Viking ***navigators***, followed by Basque, French and English fishermen, came to take advantage of the province's underwater riches. Today, fishing continues to have a very important place in the lives of the 516000 people living in Newfoundland and Labrador. The province has its own unique ***culture*** that attracts hundreds of thousands of visitors from around the world.

Did you know?

It was in 1901 at Signal Hill, in St. John's, that Italy's Guglielmo Marconi succeeded in receiving the first radio message transmitted across the Atlantic Ocean.

Labrador Sea

Quebec

A giant ***hydroelectric*** project has been developed near **Churchill Falls**.

Churchill Falls

Labrador City and **Wabush** are the province's largest iron ***producers***.

Wabush

Labrador City

A Viking village

More than a thousand years ago, the Vikings built three longhouses and five smaller buildings out of wood and sod at what is now called L'Anse aux Meadows. These great adventurers were the first Europeans to settle in North America.

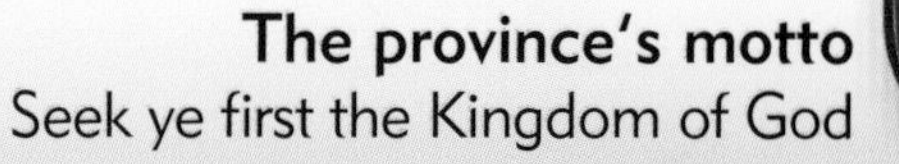
The province's motto
Seek ye first the Kingdom of God

A vanished people

The Beothuk lived along the coasts of Newfoundland. Seals, whales, fish and shellfish were their main source of food. When Europeans came to fish the rich waters, the Beothuk were driven into the interior. Disease and starvation overtook them. By 1829, the entire population was wiped out.

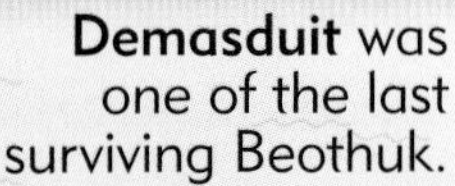

Demasduit was one of the last surviving Beothuk.

The fishing industry

The province's ***economy*** used to be based on cod fishing. A few years ago, Canada banned cod fishing off Newfoundland and Labrador because this fish was in danger of extinction. Today, the province is the biggest supplier of coldwater shrimp in the world.

St. John's is the capital of the province as well as the largest city.

Long ago, 135 root cellars were built into the grassy hillsides at **Elliston**. These caves were once used to store vegetables and to keep meat cool.

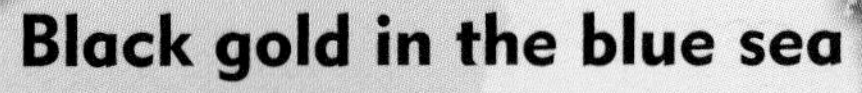

Black gold in the blue sea

There are huge petroleum deposits under the Grand Banks of Newfoundland. Hibernia, the heaviest drilling platform in the world, has been set up on one of these deposits. It is the width of two football fields and as tall as a 75-storey building.

Northwest Territories

Yukon

Nunavut

Frozen landscapes

Canada has three territories: Yukon, the Northwest Territories and Nunavut. These are cold lands with harsh ***climates*** and short summers. The landscapes in the territories are varied. To the south, the land is covered in dense ***conifer*** forest, dotted with lakes and rivers. Heading north, the trees disappear and give way to snow and the frozen waters of the Arctic. In the east, there are mountains and rocky landscapes. The central part consists of vast plains, while spectacular mountains rise in the west, creating vistas of stunning beauty.

The **Mackenzie River** is the longest river in Canada (4241 kilometres).

Mount Logan is the highest peak in Canada (5959 metres).

Kluane National Park in Yukon is a refuge for one of the largest groups of grizzly bears in North America.

Great Bear Lake is the largest lake entirely in Canada. It is the eighth-largest lake in the world.

Origin of Yukon's name
Yukon comes from the word *Yu-kun-ah*. In the native Gwich'in language, it means "great river."

lazulite

common raven

fireweed

subalpine fir

Did you know?

Wood Buffalo National Park is home to the largest herds of wild bison in the world.

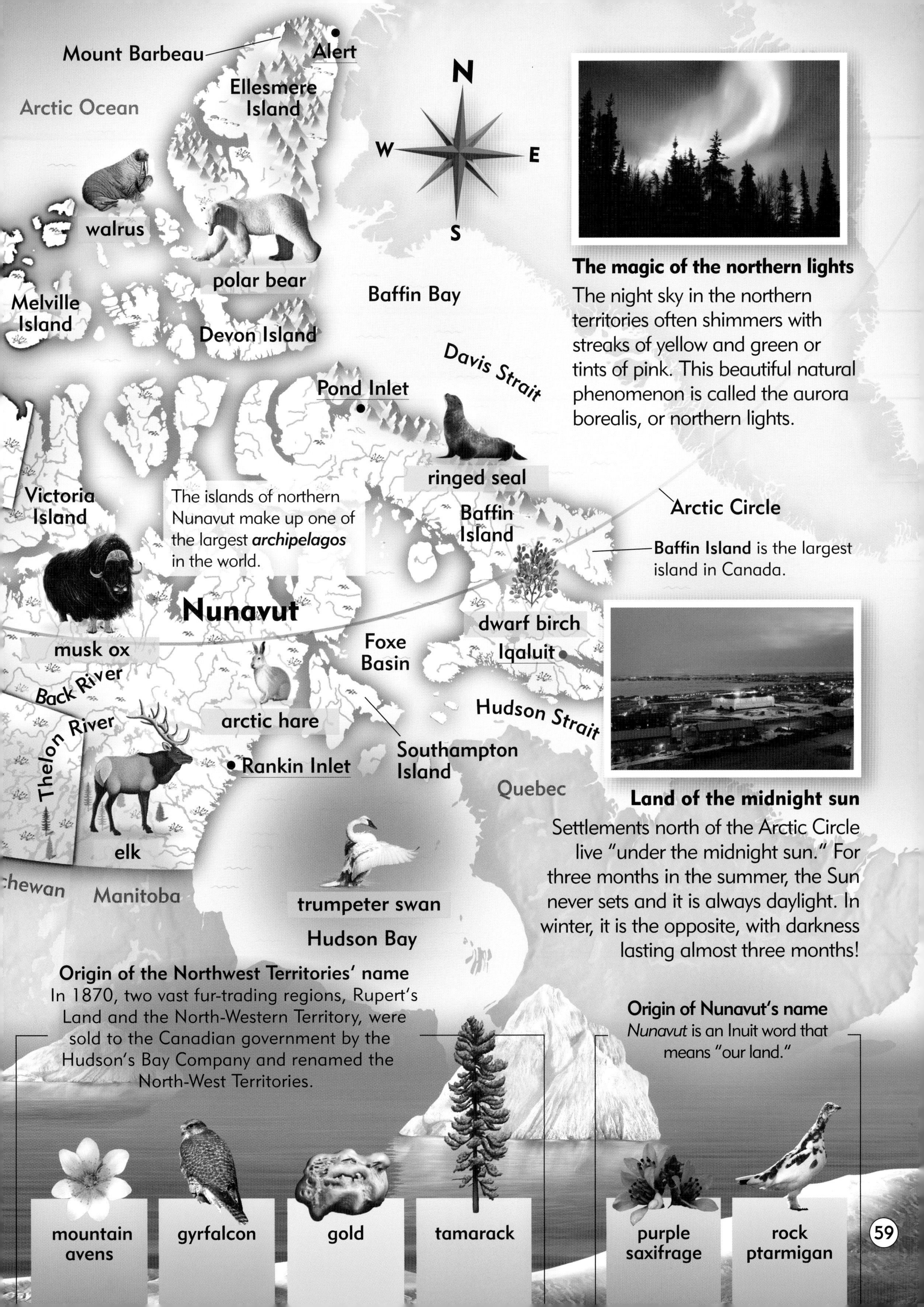

The islands of northern Nunavut make up one of the largest ***archipelagos*** in the world.

Baffin Island is the largest island in Canada.

The magic of the northern lights

The night sky in the northern territories often shimmers with streaks of yellow and green or tints of pink. This beautiful natural phenomenon is called the aurora borealis, or northern lights.

Land of the midnight sun

Settlements north of the Arctic Circle live "under the midnight sun." For three months in the summer, the Sun never sets and it is always daylight. In winter, it is the opposite, with darkness lasting almost three months!

Origin of the Northwest Territories' name

In 1870, two vast fur-trading regions, Rupert's Land and the North-Western Territory, were sold to the Canadian government by the Hudson's Bay Company and renamed the North-West Territories.

Origin of Nunavut's name

Nunavut is an Inuit word that means "our land."

Northern traditions

Canada's three territories have a distinct northern *culture*. The many Native people who live here feel a deep spiritual connection to the land. Hunting, fishing and the fur trade are major economic activities for the North's inhabitants. Many are employed in forestry, tourism and the petroleum and mining *industries*. Often people from other parts of Canada move temporarily to the territories to work. The cold *climate* is not suitable for farming, so fruits and vegetables must be shipped in from other parts of the country.

Gold!

Gold nuggets were found in the Klondike River more than 100 years ago. This discovery brought hordes of adventurers who invaded the Yukon in search of the precious metal.

Banks Island

Inuvik

United States

Dawson

Dawson was the heart of the gold rush.

Yukon

Northwest Territories

Whitehorse

Behchoko

Yellowknife

Hay River

Fort Smith

British Columbia

Alberta

Whitehorse is the capital of Yukon and home to more than 70% of its people.

Did you know?

The people of Nunavut live in isolated *communities* unconnected by roads. However, each settlement has a harbour and a small airport.

Yellowknife is the capital and the only city in the Northwest Territories.

Northwest Territories motto (none)

Yukon's motto (none)

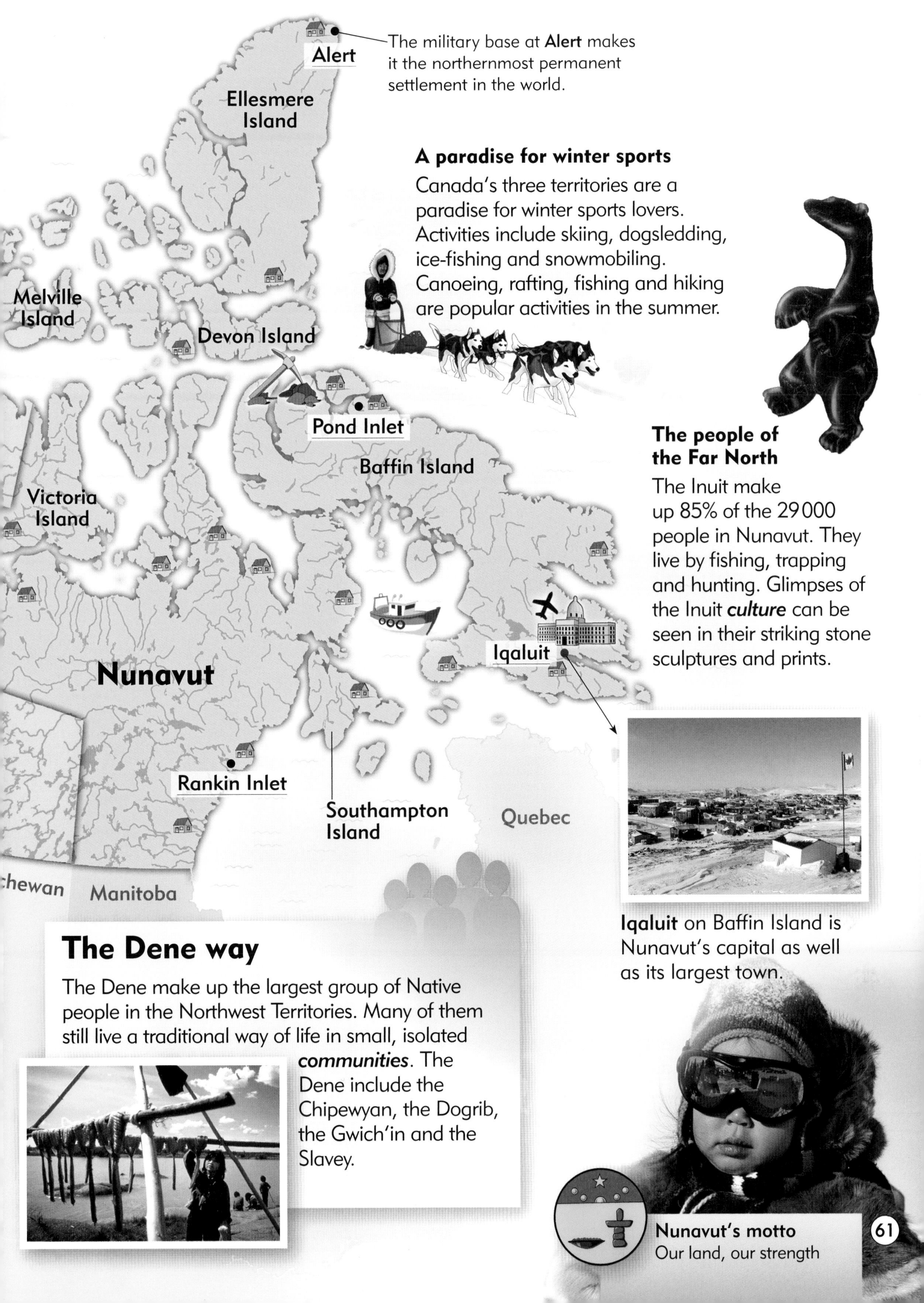

A paradise for winter sports

Canada's three territories are a paradise for winter sports lovers. Activities include skiing, dogsledding, ice-fishing and snowmobiling. Canoeing, rafting, fishing and hiking are popular activities in the summer.

The people of the Far North

The Inuit make up 85% of the 29 000 people in Nunavut. They live by fishing, trapping and hunting. Glimpses of the Inuit ***culture*** can be seen in their striking stone sculptures and prints.

Iqaluit on Baffin Island is Nunavut's capital as well as its largest town.

The Dene way

The Dene make up the largest group of Native people in the Northwest Territories. Many of them still live a traditional way of life in small, isolated ***communities***. The Dene include the Chipewyan, the Dogrib, the Gwich'in and the Slavey.

Nunavut's motto
Our land, our strength

Facts about Canada

The area of Canada
9 984 670 km^2

The area of the provinces		
1	Quebec	1 542 056 km^2
2	Ontario	1 076 395 km^2
3	British Columbia	944 735 km^2
4	Alberta	661 848 km^2
5	Saskatchewan	651 036 km^2
6	Manitoba	647 797 km^2
7	Newfoundland and Labrador	405 212 km^2
8	New Brunswick	72 908 km^2
9	Nova Scotia	55 284 km^2
10	Prince Edward Island	5660 km^2

The area of the territories		
1	Nunavut	2 093 190 km^2
2	Northwest Territories	1 346 106 km^2
3	Yukon	482 443 km^2

Where the land meets the sea

Canada has the longest coastline in the world. Counting the shores of its islands, there are about 202 080 kilometres of coastline. If we could extend this into one long line, it would circle Earth six times!

Tick-tock, tick-tock

A time zone is an area in which all clocks are set to the same hour. Canada extends over six time zones. When it is 8:00 a.m. in British Columbia, it is 9:00 a.m. in Alberta, 10:00 a.m. in Manitoba, 11:00 a.m. in Quebec, 12:00 p.m. in Nova Scotia and 12:30 p.m. in Newfoundland.

High in the sky

Toronto's First Canadian Place is the tallest office building in Canada. It stands 290 metres high and has 72 storeys.

The population of Canada
32 270 500

The population of the provinces and territories		
1	Ontario	12 541 400
2	Quebec	7 598 100
3	British Columbia	4 254 500
4	Alberta	3 256 800
5	Manitoba	1 177 600
6	Saskatchewan	994 100
7	Nova Scotia	937 900
8	New Brunswick	752 000
9	Newfoundland and Labrador	516 000
10	Prince Edward Island	138 100
11	Northwest Territories	43 000
12	Yukon	31 000
13	Nunavut	30 000

Major lakes and mountain ranges

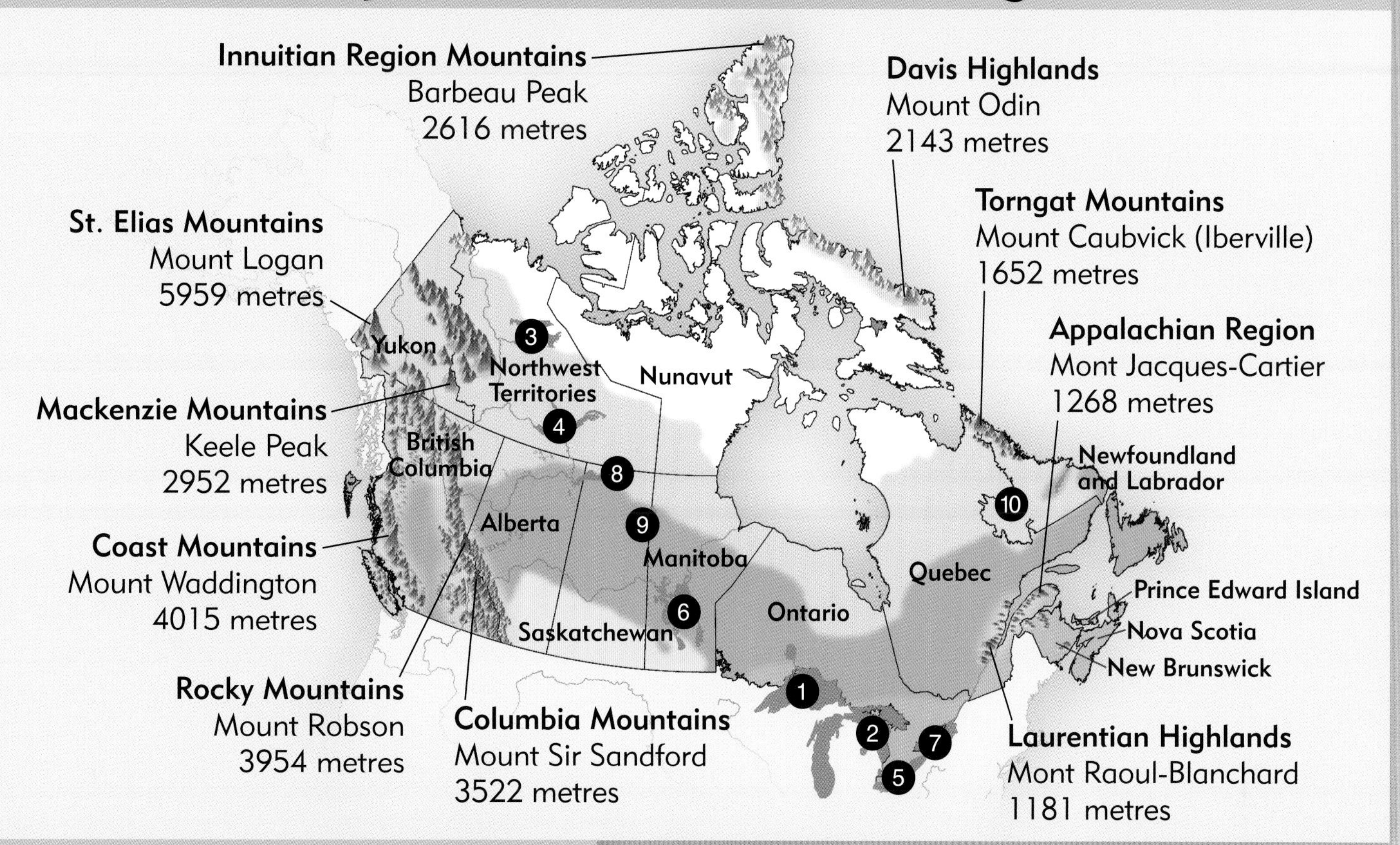

The 10 largest lakes

1	Lake Superior	82 100 km^2
2	Lake Huron	59 600 km^2
3	Great Bear Lake	31 328 km^2
4	Great Slave Lake	28 568 km^2
5	Lake Erie	25 700 km^2
6	Lake Winnipeg	24 387 km^2
7	Lake Ontario	18 960 km^2
8	Lake Athabasca	7935 km^2
9	Reindeer Lake	6650 km^2
10	Smallwood Reservoir	6527 km^2

The 10 most populated urban regions

Toronto region (Ontario, p. 36-37)	5 304 100
Montreal region (Quebec, p. 40-41)	3 635 700
Vancouver region (British Columbia, p. 20-21)	2 208 300
Ottawa-Gatineau region (Ontario/Quebec, p. 36-37, 40-41)	1 148 800
Calgary region (Alberta, p. 24-25)	1 060 300
Edmonton region (Alberta, p. 24-25)	1 016 000
Quebec City region (Quebec, p. 40-41)	717 600
Hamilton region (Ontario, p. 36-37)	714 900
Winnipeg region (Manitoba, p. 32-33)	706 900
London region (Ontario, p. 36-37)	464 300

Extreme temperatures

Canada has huge differences in temperature from one region to another and from one season to the next. The lowest temperature ever recorded was in Snag, Yukon. On February 3, 1947, it was –62.8°C. The highest temperature ever recorded was in southern Saskatchewan. On July 5, 1937, it was 45°C!

On the road

The Trans-Canada Highway is the longest highway in the world. It crosses Canada from coast to coast and measures 7821 kilometres long!

Terminology

A

agricultural
To do with cultivating the soil and rearing animals.

archipelago
A group of islands.

C

climate
The set of weather conditions common to a region.

colonist
A person who has left his/her country of origin to live in a colony.

colony
A region that is governed by a foreign country.

combustible
Capable of burning.

community
A group of people who live in the same place and share the same interests.

conifer
A tree with needles for leaves and cones for fruit. Also known as an evergreen.

culture
A set of traits particular to a community. This includes language, arts, lifestyle, group and individual rights, values, traditions and beliefs.

E

economy
A system for producing and using goods and services.

F

fjord
A long, narrow, steep-sided inlet of the sea.

fortification
A structure built to protect a settlement.

fossil
The remains or imprint of an animal or plant that lived in prehistoric times.

francophone
A person who speaks French in everyday life.

H

hydroelectric
Producing electricity using water as the power source (a waterfall or waterway).

I

immigrant
A person who has come to live in a new country.

industry
A business that converts raw materials into finished products.

islander
A person who lives on an island.

M

marshes
Land that is partially covered in water and overgrown with vegetation.

migrating
Moving from one area to another.

migratory flyway
A path that certain birds or insects take when migrating.

mineral
A precious or useful substance removed from the earth by mining.

mountain range
A line of connected mountains.

N

navigator
A person who directs the course of a ship.

P

producer
A person or business that creates goods or materials.

R

radioactive
Emitting radiation.

reservoir
A pond or a lake, natural or man-made, that is used to store water.

resources
Materials that are useful to a community.

S

species
A group of animals or plants that share common traits and that are capable of reproducing among themselves.

V

vegetation
The plants that grow in a particular area.